Boy Soldier

BOY SOLDIER

A German Teenager at the Nazi Twilight

GERHARDT B. THAMM

McFarland & Company, Inc., Publishers
Jefferson, North Carolina, and London

The present work is a reprint of the library bound edition of Boy Soldier: A German Teenager at the Nazi Twilight, *first published in 2000 by McFarland.*

Library of Congress Cataloguing-in-Publication Data

Thamm, Gerhardt B., 1930–
    Boy soldier : a German teenager at the Nazi twilight / Gerhardt B. Thamm.
        p.   cm.
    Includes bibliographical references and index.

    ISBN-13: 978-0-7864-3111-3 ∞
    (softcover : 50# alkaline paper)

    1. Thamm, Gerhardt B., 1930–   2. Soldiers — Germany — Biography.   3. World War, 1939–1945 — Personal narratives, German.   4. World War, 1939–1945 — Germany.   5. National socialism and youth.   I. Title.

D811.T4386   2007
940.54'8243 — dc21   99-53098

British Library Cataloguing-in-Publication data are available

©2000 Gerhardt B. Thamm. All rights reserved

No part of this book may be reproduced or transmitted in any form or by any means, electronic or mechanical, including photocopying or recording, or by any information storage and retrieval system, without permission in writing from the publisher.

On the cover: The author one year after his Soviet imprisonment; (inset) unidentified German soldiers

Manufactured in the United States of America

McFarland & Company, Inc., Publishers
  Box 611, Jefferson, North Carolina 28640
    www.mcfarlandpub.com

To my dear wife, Suanne,
who encouraged me to write this story;

and to all the young boy soldiers
whose dreams of glory became ashes
on the funeral pyre of the Third Reich

Contents

Preface   1
Prologue   5

PART ONE : THE WAY IT HAD BEEN   7

PART TWO : ON THE HOME FRONT   17
    1 — 1939   19
    2 — 1940   24
    3 — 1941   32
    4 — 1942   39
    5 — 1943   42
    6 — 1944   55
    7 — 1945   70

PART THREE : GÖTTERDÄMMERUNG (APOCALYPSE)   75
    8 — The Omen   77
    9 — Distant Thunder   82
    10 — Flight   87
    11 — Retreat into the Sudeten Mountains   96

PART FOUR : BOY SOLDIERS   103
    12 — Oh, to Be a Soldier   105
    13 — Sergeant "One-Eye"   107

14 — Frontline Duty		111
15 — The "Forgotten Front"		125
16 — The Russian Boy		132
17 — "Routine" Patrol		139
18 — Ah, Natascha		143
19 — To the Bitter End		151

Postscript: Strangers in Their Own Land   159
Notes   169
Index   175

Preface

As I perused the Autumn 1996 issue of the *Wilson Quarterly* I found a quote by Paul Fussell, a professor of English at the University of Pennsylvania and "a superannuated, badly wounded, former infantry lieutenant," whose experiences seemed particularly apropos to my experience as a boy soldier long ago in a faraway place. Fussell wrote that

> The truth is that very few people know anything about war. In an infantry division, for example, fewer than half of the troops actually fight, that is, fight with rifles, mortars, machine guns, grenades, and trench knives. The others, thousands upon thousands of them, are occupied with ... housekeeping tasks.... For those unlucky enough to be in the forward combat units, the war meant death or maiming, usually in extraordinarily dirty and undignified circumstances. At the very least, for most it meant a rapid and shocking metamorphosis from boyhood innocence to adult cynicism and bitterness.... Tolstoy's words are worth recalling: "War," he said, "is not a polite recreation, but the vilest thing in life, and we ought to understand that and not play at war."[1]

To those of us who fought in World War Two against the Soviets it seemed that war on the Western Front was conducted in a relatively "gentlemanly" way. On the Eastern Front war was fought bitterly, with atrocities committed on all sides. From East Prussia, later from east of the Oder River, came reports of horrible atrocities. Nazi leaders must share the blame for the death and depravation of hundreds of thousands of civilians in East Prussia, and several million in Silesia. They failed to initiate timely evacuation orders because every member of the Nazi party, at every echelon of the party structure, feared to be called a "defeatist." A defeatist could be summarily executed for his "sins," i.e., hung from the nearest lamp post by other, more zealous, Nazis. Notified entirely too late, terrified women and children fled westward in every imaginable conveyance. They clogged all roads with slow-moving civilian horse- and oxen-drawn covered wagons, handcarts, bicycles, etc. The refugee flow impeded the movement of Wehrmacht elements rushing to set up defensive positions. Where Soviet tanks caught up with these refugee *Treks* (wagon trains) their tanks ran over horses and wagons loaded with women and children. We, the few, who tried to delay, to save, to stave off annihilation did not always succeed — but we surely tried.

As a fifteen-year-old boy I fought briefly in a war. My fight was neither noble nor heroic. I saw the horrors that no fifteen-year-old boy should ever see. I came into war purely by unfortunate happenstance, and survived it purely by lucky coincidence. The unfortunate happenstance? On an afternoon in February 1945 Soviet forces of the 1st Ukrainian Front attacked and captured my home town. On that day I lost my home and many friends and acquaintances. Neighbors who had not fled suffered incredible terror. Arbitrary executions were common. They were raped, tortured, or killed; some suffered many years in Siberian prisons. Most died. One man was shot because he had ration stamps with swastikas in his wallet, yet all official state documents were adorned with swastikas. Rape and murder were everyday occurrences. One of our neighbors, Herr Arnold, a tobacco store owner and ardent anti–Hitlerite, stayed behind to pass out cigars and cigarettes to his Soviet "liberators." He was shot by one of the liberators riding on a tank. Our family's butcher, Herr Ritter, was shot when he tried to prevent the rape of one of his salesgirls. Mrs. Anna Walter, who lived in a house just north of my grandfather's farm, fainted after being raped numerous times. The Russians threw her into the bathtub, ran cold water to revive her, then raped her again. When she again fainted she was dispatched with three shots. Small girls, adult women, and grandmothers were raped repeatedly; many were then shot or committed suicide. Other horrors, too terrible to describe here, are recorded in Rolf Becker's book.[2] Three months later it became our sad task to bury the decaying bodies of these unfortunates who were left wherever they died.

According to official reports of the *Bundesministerium für Vertriebene* (the German Refugee Ministry), of a total population of 4,578,000 in Niederschlesien (Lower Silesia) 1.5 million were overrun and captured by Soviet forces during battle, 3.2 million fled, and every sixth person, 874,000 in all, was killed. Those who were overrun by the Soviets suffered what British historian Albert Seaton described as "the most fearful barbarity and atrocity."[3] They were the innocent, the old, the infirm, the sick, the too young. The guilty, the Nazi party bosses, the executioners, the concentration camp managers had fled long before to escape Soviet retribution. They had left their charges to face the bitter consequences.

Maybe, just maybe, I fought in this war to escape this "most fearful barbarity and atrocity." Maybe I wrote this account to still the memories.

> Gerhardt B. Thamm
> Fernandina Beach, Florida
> Summer 1999

Prologue

> *What kind of land is this,*
> *Our Silesia,*
> *For which torrents of blood*
> *were sacrificed*
> *For which bitter tears*
> *were spilled?*
> *It is Germany's richest*
> *and most beautiful*
> *eastern land.[1]*

Toward the east, far beyond the horizon, cold, blue-white fingers caressed the winter sky. Once or twice a tiny firefly-like glitter appeared; then two, three, or four of the bright searchlight cones converged mercilessly on the twisting and turning aircraft. A slender fourteen-year-old boy leaned against the rough stone wall near the double-winged back door of his grandfather's farmhouse, his dark, curly hair hidden under a fur cap, flaps securely tied under his chin to protect his ears from the bitter cold. Although wrapped in heavy winter gear, a steady, ice-cold easterly from the Polish plains penetrated even the heaviest of clothing. He stood in almost total darkness. The wartime blackout was complete. Only the silver sliver of the moon cast a cold light on the buildings. Its light reflected from the thick blanket of snow that covered everything, casting mysterious shadows here and there. The boy could barely discern the dark outlines of the fieldstone barn that formed one of the sides of what had once been a small outpost fort guarding the northwestern gate of Jauer, a small town that he called home in the eastern province of Lower Silesia in the hinterlands of Germany. Beyond the farm's back gate he saw the bare outlines of the snow-covered road that led into the fields of the farm.

It was early January 1945. The boy listened to the familiar noises: the reports that echoed like pistol shots when the ice expanded on the shallow pond, the snorts from restless horses in the dark stable across the farmyard, and the lonely howls from Doberman guard dogs at the rendering plant at the edge of town. It was as it had always been, only now the probing cones of concentrated light reminded him that beyond the horizon friends and foes were dying in the air raid on Breslau, the state capital.

Slowly, first one, then another, and finally all the searchlights disappeared. He stood a long time watching as the silent light spectacle slowly faded into the dark winter sky. He waited until the steady wail of the siren atop the city hall tower signaled the end of danger from above. The boy listened once more, but all was quiet. The horses too were now silent, even the Dobermans had ceased their mournful howling. It was late. Tomorrow would come news of the successful defense of Breslau, and later, trains, loaded with wounded from the Eastern Front, would again arrive to be unloaded. The boy turned; he thought, *Better get a good night's sleep.*

I opened the heavy door and shouted into the silent blacked-out hall, "It's over. They have gone. End of raid." Now the murmur of relieved voices came from the kitchen where everyone had waited under its vaulted ceiling, the strongest part of the house. Grandfather, a dour, skinny man in his late sixties, always dressed in a brown, herringbone, three-piece suit, rasped, "The Breslauers really got it tonight. Wonder what they did to deserve that?" One of my young cousins asked, "*Opa*,[2] what would happen if a bomb dropped here?" Grandfather, a veteran of the First World War and the only one in the house with any war experience, laughed, "Those bombers? They couldn't find Jauer if they tried. From that high up, and at night, they are lucky if they find Breslau."

With that all felt better.

PART ONE

The Way It Had Been

My grandfather's farm originally had been an outpost fort. Once there were four of these forts, each guarding one of the city gates. In earlier days the occupants of the fort had the lonely mission of getting invaders and marauders — and there were many — into a cross fire of arrows between it and the city gate. Sometimes they were successful, often they were not and suffered bitter consequences. Only the one on Vorwerkstrasse,[1] my grandfather's, had survived urbanization and become a part of the town. A mountain stream, the Wütende Neisse, meandered, at times thundered, from the Sudeten Mountains, through the foothills, past Jauer into the flatlands of Lower Silesia. Some thirty mountainous miles to the south lay Czechoslovakia, and fifty miles across the fertile Silesian plains was the Polish frontier. About 13,500 souls lived in Jauer in relative harmony. They farmed the surrounding fields, harvested timber, built horse-drawn wagons, manufactured farm implements, baked good bread, and made excellent spicy sausage, the renowned *Jauersche Würstel*.

My German and Polish ancestors had lived here before learned people had invented that terrible word "nation-state" that had brought so much strife during the past few centuries. Together they had fought against the Mongol hordes at Wahlstatt near Liegnitz on 9 April 1241. It was here, according to legend, that the German wife of Polish Duke Henry II avenged his death by leading the survivors of the battle against the Mongols. At least, that is what we wanted to believe. History records that the Mongols departed for reasons of internal politics — but the myth lives on. In the 1350s, when Silesia became part of the Holy Roman empire, my Slavic and Germanic ancestors became citizens of that empire. Later, in the thirty-year war, they fought against Swedish, German, and Hungarian marauders. For some time Silesia was part of the Austro-Hungarian empire. When Frederick the Great, after many years of conflict, finally defeated the armies of Empress Maria-Theresa of Austria in the mid–1740s Silesia became part of the kingdom of Prussia. The French occupied Jauer from 1807 to 1812. Field Marshal Blücher, commanding Prussian and Russian troops, defeated the French in 1812 in the battle on the Katzbach River, just a few miles down the road west of town.

Through these many centuries the citizens of Jauer survived, licked their wounds, regrouped, and prospered. With our blood lines already a mixture of Poles, Bohemians, and citizens from many German principalities, our ancestors had first become good, solid Silesians, then Austrians, later Prussians, and later yet, fiercely loyal Germans. However, as a remnant of our Slavic past our Silesian-German dialect still has the harsh Slavic *r*, harsher than the more "acceptable" German spoken elsewhere, and our sentence structure shows influences of our Slavic past.

An ever so slight topographic depression protected Jauer somewhat from the ice-cold Siberian winds blowing across the Polish plains. Travelers approaching from any direction first saw the narrow steeple of city hall with its distinctive, triple onion-shaped cupola. Then the dark gray fortress-like tower of the Catholic St. Martin Church beckoned the wanderer defiantly. Those approaching from the south encountered the massive walls of the Piasten[2] Palace which protected those approaches to the town.

Jauer's citizens were not shy about telling visitors that their town was the smallest in Germany with a 200-year tradition of repertoire performances; they were especially proud of the theater's beautiful baroque interior. The theater lay partly hidden at the rear of the city hall, a complex of buildings in the central plaza that also housed a pharmacy, several stores, the city police station, and, as in most German towns, a fine restaurant — the Rathskeller.

During the many centuries of its existence the town had outgrown its narrow, curving streets which followed the contour of the outer defensive wall. As a reminder of its turbulent past a remnant of the breastworks stood preserved for posterity. With the expansion of the city came wide, tree-lined streets, city parks, and a charming railroad station. An old military barracks, formerly of the 154th Silesian Infantry Regiment, had long ago been converted into low-income apartments. A modern garrison was enlarged to more than twice its original size during the mid–1930s; during that time it became the home of the 83rd Silesian Infantry Regiment and my father's 461st Silesian Infantry Regiment (Reserve).

Jauer's citizens were also proud of their spicy sausages, produced there since 1340, and the world-renowned *Bienenkörbe*—creations of sweet macaroons, cakes made of eggs, sugar, almonds, and flour shaped into beehives; each had little sugar bees hanging on the shell. The beehives came in various sizes, up to three feet in height. Its creator, a local baker, told anyone willing to listen that one of his large beehives was presented to Franklin Delano Roosevelt on his first inauguration as president of the United States. There was also the famous horse carriage, the *Jauerwagen*—the first carriage where the horse was guided from inside the cab; the Mennonites in Pennsylvania are still using similar carriages today. The citizens were proud of their town. They promoted these specialties in songs and by word-of-mouth. They shared a mystical love for the soil they cultivated, the songs they sang, and the tunes to which they danced. They loved the dark, pine-covered *Blauen Berge*, the dark-blue Sudeten Mountains, the little cottages hidden in deep green valleys. During the long winter evenings their children listened to wonderful stories of the mischievous giant Rübezahl and the gnomes who helped him in his never-ending endeavor to expose haughtiness, arrogance, and condescension; Rübezahl ridiculed and punished them all.

Sitting in our large kitchen with its strong walls and its low, vaulted ceiling we listened enchanted to these tales. With air raid alerts becoming ever more frequent, the kitchen, the strongest part of the house, had become our air raid shelter. Centuries ago it had been the core of the small fort that stood guard before the city gate, thus the name: *Vorwerk* (outer fort). It had been an austere structure with thick walls of native granite. The fort had apparently only three ground-level strong rooms; the tower was later torn down during one of many "modernizations." One of the essentials of an outpost fort was a deep well for potable water; in modern times the cool waters of that well below one of the strong rooms kept fresh the farm's milk.

During the past five centuries the farm had been modified many times. Previous owners had added huge stone barns and stables. Because little thought had been given to some of those alterations the center hall was in perpetual darkness lit only marginally by two widely spaced low-wattage lamps. Water crept up the stone walls and, no matter how often the mason tried, the mortar would not stay on the walls of Grandfather's ground level everyday living room. Large, hard, granite slabs formed the stairs leading to the second floor. Many generations of children, and some of their elders, had suffered scraped elbows or knees tripping on these stairs.

My grandfather's farm consisted of five two-story buildings. They formed a large rectangle. The two-story residence, with its large, two-story attic, had all the comforts of the city and many of the pleasures associated with country living. There was running water, a modern sewer system, and city gas, even electric lights. City sidewalks made the ten-minute walk to the center of town a pure pleasure. The residence and a large stable with two floors for grain storage above, faced southward. Passersby viewed the residence through a wrought-iron fence and some 200 feet of gardens. A cobblestone driveway and sidewalk separated the residence from the other large building that faced the street. An ancient, large, double-winged wrought-iron gate for wagon traffic, with an equally impressive gate for pedestrians, guarded the residence from casual intruders. The gate, painted some time ago with expensive black oil paint, exhibited wear and tear, indicative of the wartime paint shortage for civilian use. The walls of the residence were of now-faded yellow stucco, the barns and stables of rough, gray stucco. Heavy timbers supported the dark, bluish-gray tiled roof of the residence and the red clay tiles of the barns and stables. Viewing it from the street, there was something indefinably romantic, sturdy, everlasting about that farm.

Under the slate roof of the residence the wonderful aroma of apples and pears stored during the winter permeated the high, two-story gabled attic. On rainy days laundry hung there on long hemp lines to dry. For me the attic was a treasure chest of family history. My grandfather's uniforms were there—those wonderful dress uniforms, colorful military caps and helmets; reminders of days long gone, days of splendor and romance, of glory and victory. Grandfather had served in the kaiser's 154th Silesian Infantry Regiment before and during the "Great War" as he called World War One. Otto and Arthur, his two eldest sons, had joined the regiment during the last year of that war. The attic's large oaken closets held the dress uniforms and the colorful helmet of leather and brass Grandfather had worn before World War One, and the steel helmets and field uniforms he and his sons wore during that war.

Peeking through the porthole-like windows near the attic floor one saw the gardens that surrounded the entire estate. A park-like flower garden segregated the residence from the public street. Thick rose and lilac bushes screened the park from public view. A low stone wall topped with a wrought-iron fence enclosed the park. A large vegetable garden separated the garage, stables, and grain storage building from the city street. To the east a fieldstone wall and a fence screened the farm from a neighbor's villa. To the west another stone wall screened the large fruit tree orchard from the public; there horses and heifers grazed in rich, deep grass. From the back of the farm a private dirt road led for almost two miles northward through the fields of the *Lehngut*— the ancient term for an estate that paid no taxes, but whose landlord owed direct service to the king of Prussia and emperor of Germany. Large old chestnut trees to the left and right of Vorwerkstrasse formed a pleasant green tunnel during spring, summer, and autumn. When winter storms raged from the Sudeten Mountains, or swept drifting snow from the Polish plains, the bare, black branches beckoned in an almost threatening manner. Before the war a lone gas lamp had cast its flickering light onto the street. Now, with wartime blackout, there was only darkness.

The farm had withstood time, war, and, at times, negligence. My grandfather bought it from a bankrupt gambling nobleman who died by his own hand in the grain loft. It was whispered that on stormy nights when there was a new moon, the nobleman's ghost wandered through the barns with a rope hanging from his withered hand. Our maids refused to fetch firewood from a storage room in that barn during the evening hours. The residence, the oldest part of the fort, had vaulted ceilings and thick, rough, stone walls in places five to six feet deep; so thick that in earlier days I and my cousin played comfortably on the window sills.

I had lived on my grandfather's city farm as far back as I could remember. It was a wonderful old place with many nooks and crannies where children could play hide and seek. My cousins and I, my schoolmate Lothar Scholz,[3] and his sister, Susi, had spent many happy afternoons in the courtyard, orchards, barns, stables, and granary playing as well as doing the many chores associated with farm work. Lothar's and Susi's father was a local policeman in charge of price controls for our little town and nearby villages. The family lived in one of two upper-floor apartments that my ever-frugal grandfather leased to non–family members. Lothar, Susi, and I attended the town's middle school less than half a mile from the farm. Lothar was almost one year older than I, but we attended the same class. Susi was in our companion class; there were separate classes for boys and girls. Boys and girls could meet only during class breaks, and then only in the schoolyard. There the boys and girls would cast furtive glances at each other. The teachers thought that any closer association would lead to a general deterioration of morals. Little did they know.

Life for those living in Jauer in the prelude to World War Two seemed to have improved enormously. Just a few years before there had been widespread unemployment. But now the depression had ended. Germany had overcome the psychologically demeaning *Versailles Diktat*, the Nazi party's description of the peace treaty that had terminated the World War. Germans once again looked with confidence into a bright future. Now, in this rather tranquil year of 1938, even non–party members such as my father were gainfully employed. Although we were still living on my grandfather's farm — poor people with many children had priority for government-sponsored housing — there were prospects of getting a city government employee apartment in a few years. Most important: Father had just started to work at the local Labor Office. The position paid him enough to support his family comfortably. I remember one glorious Saturday afternoon in the early summer of 1938 when Father proudly brought home a used Siemens-Halski radio. It was in excellent condition, with long, medium, and short wave bands (there was no UHF wave band in those days). Every Saturday afternoon I met Father at his office and every Saturday from that day forth he and I bought the magazine *Hör zu!* at the newsstand; it had the schedule of the next week's radio programs.

There may have been dark clouds on the horizon, but in Jauer it looked as if our family would come into its own. The winter, at least the way I remember it, was snowy and cold, but in Jauer every winter was snowy and cold. With the New Year just starting, the snow was about one to two feet deep. In Jauer the snow stayed on the ground until spring. The sidewalks received a light sprinkle of ashes so one would not slip on the ice; there was no salt to melt the ice. Until spring it was quiet in Jauer; the snow muffled all the usual noises from horse-drawn wagons and horses' hoofs. I continued grammar school in the *Alte Schule* right behind the *Friedhof*, the Protestant cemetery, the same school Father had attended from 1909 to 1917.

Spring, when it finally arrived, was the most beautiful time of the year. First the *Schneeglöckchen*— snowbells — poked their heads through the crusty snow. Shortly thereafter crocuses started to bloom. The spring

Cemetery gate. Below: "Thought of the day: 'He whom love overwhelms, eats and sleeps less.'" *Author's diary.*

flowers below our window were always the first to bloom because our room faced south. One of the big events, for children, was *Sommersingen*, summer caroling. Each child had a stick crowned by a small wreath; inside the wreath was a little yellow or pink bird. Long colorful paper ribbons streamed from the bottom of the wreath. From house to house we went, singing in our Silesian dialect silly little songs of endearment — and our neighbors filled the baskets with small candies.

Part Two

On the Home Front

Chapter 1

1939

National and international events did somewhat disturb our tranquility. When Hitler marched into Bohemia and Moravia on 15–16 March 1939, young Czechoslovakia, the country just a few miles south of our little town, ceased to exist as a nation. In May 1939 the Legion Condor, German "volunteers" who had fought for Spain's Franco to defeat the "communist menace," returned victorious. For some years I saved a copy of *Der Adler*, a German Air Force magazine. On its front page was a handsome German pilot in the unique Legion Condor uniform with the Spanish red-gold-red flag in the background. We were quite proud to have beaten back Communism in Spain.

As summer approached, we heard stories about mistreatment, even killings of Germans living in Poland. Preuss *Oma*[1] and my mother were worried because most of their relatives, all farmers and sheepherders, lived in the former German province of Posen; which became Poland in 1919. It had been the home of Preuss Oma's family for centuries. Mother and all her siblings were born there, but when that part of the former German empire became Poland Preuss Opa, a federal employee, had to move into post–World War One Germany so as not to forfeit his retirement. Thus, one part of the Preuss family came to Jauer.

But with the beginning of the summer harvest farmers were less concerned with international events; their main concern was inclement weather that could ruin their crops. The *Vorwerkgut* was a beehive of activity. We were no longer directly involved with farm work since Father no longer worked on the farm. Nevertheless, I enjoyed being with horses and going into the fields. During the difficult years of unemployment, when Father still worked on my grandfather's farm, he would lift me atop one of the plow horses as he walked them into the fields. I loved the gentle rhythm of the horses as they walked across furrows, and I loved the special smell of horses. I do not ever recall Father riding a horse; his brother Gerhard was the family's horseman.

As long tradition wanted it, as a side line my grandfather raised horses for the army. In 1939 he bought a new mare to breed. Stutti was a brownish-gray light saddle and wagon horse. She was gentle, but could be fiery at times. I groomed her often and gave her a carrot or two as a treat. She responded well to commands; when I called she obeyed readily. Walking through the pasture I enjoyed scaring my schoolmates. When I called her name she came racing toward us in full gallop and stopped just directly in front of me. My friends thought she would not stop and that a wild horse was on the loose.

We had a beautiful, warm summer. Most of our cereal crops had already been harvested and stored out of harm's way in our huge barns. Following tradition, early autumn was the time for army maneuvers. It seemed as if maneuvers had started somewhat earlier in 1939. The 83rd Silesian Infantry Regiment, our hometown regiment, was constantly on the move. Periodically troops and horses were quartered in the *Vorwerkgut*. For us children it was a lot of fun. Even the soldiers, many of whom were reservists, seemed to enjoy the break from the boring routine of civilian life.

Then, at 0445 hours on the 1st of September, German troops crossed the border into Poland. Father was called to active duty. He was the oldest enlisted man in the 461st Silesian Infantry Regiment (Reserve); only the regimental commander was older than him. His position at the Labor Office, classified as "essential to the war effort," was filled by a Nazi party member, and Father was drafted.

Father, like every other German of military age, had undergone periodic military training; he at Silesia's large Sommerfeld training area. On the 3rd of September, he stood with his fellow Silesians in the ancient garrison square. The sun, filtered by an early morning haze, cast its cold reflection on rows of gray steel helmets. Father's company made up three sides of the formation. The harsh command of their first sergeant called them to attention. The executive officer, standing at the open end of the formation, first raised, then lowered his saber between two rows of recruits representing their comrades in this solemn ceremony. Six soldiers grasped the saber's cold steel with their left hands. The flag bearer respectfully lowered his staff until the standard touched the holy soil of

Germany. Then all recruits raised their right arms high, middle and index fingers extended. Deep voices reverberated across the cobblestones and echoed through the corridors of the old stone barracks:

> I swear by God this holy oath, that I will render to Adolf Hitler, leader of the German nation and people, supreme commander of the Armed Forces, unconditional obedience, and that I am ready as a brave soldier to risk my life at any time for this oath.[2]

Thus Father and his neighbors became soldiers of the Reich. They joined what both friend and foe considered the world's best and most powerful fighting machine. He, his younger brother Gerhard, and for a very brief time his older brother Arthur, followed the hallowed tradition of service to the Fatherland in Silesia's infantry. Since the days of Frederick the Great loyalty to the Fatherland, tradition, and the finest military training had been the hallmark of this army. For over two centuries Prussian nobility had supplied the core of its officers. The strength of this army was love for the Fatherland, unbending loyalty, superb training, and harsh discipline enforced by brutal punishment. For over two centuries this army had been the instrument of national policy for kings and emperors—and now it had become the tool of one of history's most ruthless and despicable dictators.

Four days after swearing-in my father's regiment marched along Vorwerkstrasse and Bahnhofstrasse to the railroad station. Children ran alongside their fathers, handed them flowers for their uniform pockets. Upon arrival at the cobblestone plaza before the station the captain dismissed the formation for a last good-bye between his soldiers and their loved ones. Wives gave their husbands, girls their boyfriends, a last hug and kiss. Sons stood proudly next to their fathers, and daughters clutched their fathers' tunics. Then the soldiers scrambled aboard the boxcars and, with smoke and steam puffing from the engine, with whistles hooting, brass band playing, the train pulled out of the station—eastward. The crowd cheered. I waved a long good-bye as my father left to fight the war in Poland.

We knew Father and his neighbors were fighting for a just cause. For several months Herr Goebbels, Germany's propaganda minister, and his helpers had been telling us on the radio and in the newspapers that the German minorities living in Poland were being mistreated, beaten, even killed. Germany had to act to save fellow Germans. According to

Herr Goebbels, there was no choice. This was to be a short war for a just cause, the Führer had so decreed. Poland was defeated in eighteen days. Herr Goebbels' grand slogan, *In achzehn Tagen hat sie der Herr geschlagen* (In eighteen days the Lord has vanquished them), made you wonder whether *Herr* was a play on words. Did it mean our Lord God — or the Führer?

After liberation Mother's uncles and aunts confirmed Herr Goebbels' story of atrocities against Germans committed by Poles, and sanctioned by their government, but our relatives credited their own survival to their Polish neighbors who had risked their own lives in the process. Alas, the Führer, whom the German propaganda machine soon called *Der Grösste Feldherr Aller Zeiten*, i.e., the Greatest Field Marshal of All Times,[3] had miscalculated. Soon after Germany entered Poland, France and England declared war on Germany. Was this to be a replay of the Great War? We all hoped history would not repeat itself. War and war hysteria soon became an all-consuming topic. At the very beginning of the war everyone was issued a gas mask — called *Volksgasmaske* (people's gas mask). One per person, with special gas masks with hoods for mothers with infants. Grandfather even received six gas masks for his horses; he threw them contemptuously behind the feed locker in the horse stable.

With Father, his brother, and many other relatives, neighbors, and acquaintances serving in the armed forces my family eagerly followed the progression of the war. No matter how people felt about the Nazi party, every good citizen was involved in furthering the war effort; after all, our lads were fighting for the Fatherland. Teachers encouraged students to collect scrap iron, rags, even leftover bones from meals. In small towns and large cities, even in places far removed from important happenings and critical war production, wartime blackout was strictly enforced. If even the slightest sliver of light emerged from windows or doors the omnipotent air raid warden came and gave a stern warning. If it occurred more than once the violator could expect fines, and even jail time. Not even the slightest bit of light could leak from the windows of the farm; every window had sturdy wooden shutters on the inside. Thus, it was not difficult to block light and achieve total blackout. Those living in low-income housing had blinds made of cheap wartime blackout paper. They, more often than not, received warnings. In conjunction with the blackout there were placards everywhere of frightening skeletons riding bombers with slogans proclaiming *Der Feind sieht Dein Licht — Verdunkeln* (the enemy sees your light — blackout). Living in the hinterlands of Germany all this hype appeared totally unnecessary. Not until the latter stages of the war were there even air raid warnings in our peaceful corner of Germany. Only the absence of fathers and brothers, the strict food rationing, and the last page of the newspaper that carried the names of friends, acquaintances, and every so often a relative, who had "died in faraway places for Führer, Reich, and Fatherland," reminded us that we were at war.

For those living on farms, food rationing was never a real problem, but city folks received only items for which they had ration coupons. Ration cards for food were introduced at the very beginning of the war. Soon clothing, shoes (even shoelaces), soap, and laundry powder were available only in limited amounts, and only with ration stamps. There were even ration cards for horse fodder for nonfarm animals and food for dogs. There were separate ration cards for meat (blue); fat and milk products (yellow); sugar, jam, and marmalade (white); eggs (green); flour, rice, and other cereals, including *Ersatzkaffee*—roasted barley (pink); and fruits and nuts (purple). Childbearing women, coal miners, and those engaged in difficult labor received additional rations. The ration cards also served as an excellent population control measure; they were good only in the area of residence. There were special ration stamps for those traveling; the request for these stamps had to be accompanied by a police authorization certificate to travel from and to specified locations. It all seemed very restrictive and complicated, but for some of the poorer folks this was the first time they were ever able to buy butter. Violation of the rationing directives, black-marketing, was punishable with sentences up to and including death.

We suffered from the shock of being without a father, but we also were very proud. We felt superior to those few whose fathers were still civilians. Father's regiment marched through Poland; they were infantry—no trucks or trains, just soldiers marching. He said their record for one day's march was eighty kilometers. That's a long way to walk considering that they had to carry all the gear, weapons, and ammunition. Soldiers of the walking infantry coined the adage "A bad ride is better than a good walk," but in the early days of the war they walked. After the Polish campaign Father's regiment transferred to the Western Front. He went to a listening post far in front of the Westwall (the Siegfried Line) fortification. There he and his comrades dug shelters secured with thick logs. They piled much dirt on top and then camouflaged the whole structure with small pine trees.

Chapter 2

1940

The next year, 1940, started rather quietly. Father had been on Christmas leave; the German Army took good care of its men. Fathers received preference on holiday leave. He returned to the Western Front just after the new year; others, those without children, were waiting to go on leave. Today all this may seem ludicrous, but then, most of us — at least most adults — looked at the war and the government in a curious, one might even say schizophrenic, way. Grandfather for example was a royalist. He thought there was only one legitimate German ruler: the kaiser. He despised Hitler, the usurper *Gefreiter*[1]; he did not think the Nazis were too smart. But, at the same time, under that political system, our entire lives were controlled by the Nazis. They told us what to think, what and how much to eat. They even told Grandfather what and how much to plant. Most of all, the Nazis tolerated no dissent from, or criticism of, their party line. On the other hand, Grandfather would have been the last one to wish Germany ill. That would have been unpatriotic. He listened several times each day to the news broadcasts. He relished German victories. During the news broadcast we could hear him gleefully rasping, "*Na*, the lads showed those *Britischers* what we are made of."[2] I think it never occurred to him that Hitler had started that war, and that any victory would only strengthen the man he so despised. Preuss Oma, our dear, church-going grandmother, believed everything she read in our daily newspaper. It never occurred to her that lies could be printed in that journal. After all, she knew some of these local newsmen, and they were all decent people. What reasons would they have to lie to the folks in Jauer? Like most of the people around us, she was totally apolitical. This of course was the insidious aspect of people control:

the many good, totally apolitical persons, who for feelings of deep patriotism, supported the government. Even if they had become privy to some terrible happening they would have turned to each other and said, "If only the Führer knew," and automatically assume that Hitler would right the wrong.

The very few who openly condemned the Nazi party, or the way the war was conducted, were labeled traitors. Of course, they soon learned that it was not healthy to criticize either the party or the Führer. And, like Pavlov's dogs, the people had gotten used to the regime, had even gotten to like it — and supported it. In fact, most of the formerly unemployed manual workers, who at one time or other had opposed the Nazis, and had fervently supported the Social Democrats or even the Communists, now just as fervently supported the Führer and his henchmen.

My grandfather, Thamm Opa. *Author's collection.*

As one of his first moves, Hitler had built small, semidetached houses with large gardens on expropriated lands. Now, these folks, many with ten or twelve children, moved from squalid, one-room quarters into these houses. The men folk were given jobs and some were conscripted to work until they again became accustomed to the strenuous routine of day labor — "good, old German labor ethics." Their wives, having many children, were honored as "German mothers" and received the "Cross of Motherhood." There were three categories of the cross: bronze, silver, and gold. All mothers with four or more children were awarded the "Mother's Cross" at public ceremonies — and they proudly wore it on all holidays and public functions. They looked at Hitler as their savior. He had pulled them from squalor, had given them respect. Who else had ever done anything for them? All in all, it was a curious time.

In the meantime, on 1 February 1940, Father, still at the Western Front; still at a forward outpost of the Siegfried Line, and still with Jauer's 461st Infantry Regiment (Reserve), became a *Gefreiter*, and all was quiet on the Western Front until.... On the 9th of April a news flash from Reichsender[3] Breslau announced that German troops had invaded Denmark and Norway. At first no one could understand why we would even attempt to do such a foolish thing, but soon the explanation came: We beat the *Britischers* to the punch by mere hours. They had planned to occupy Norway and launch attacks on the Reich from the north. There had already been an incident in Norwegian waters when a British destroyer boarding party with Norwegian "collusion," had searched the German merchant ship *Altmark*. With the occupation of Denmark and Norway another threat against the Reich was eliminated. The radio announcer once again jubilantly reassured the folks of Jauer that the Führer had visions as no other.

As far back as I could remember, the Führer's birthday on the 20th of April was cause for celebration. All merchants decorated their store windows. In the center, the place of honor, was the largest and most expensive oil painting the shopkeeper could afford — the better, the more expensive the painting, the better German he was. All paintings portrayed Hitler looking sternly into the distance. He wore a rather plain uniform with only those medals he had won in World War One, but a military greatcoat, loosely draped over his shoulders, gave him that "fieldmarshalesque" look. Fresh pine bows and oak leaves gave the decoration that earthy, genuinely German look; black, white, and red bunting supplemented the decorations. Despite the blackout, and only on that day, large, red wax candles illuminated the entire scene. During midmorning the local garrison marched in review before the war memorial, and during the afternoon members of the fire department, the boys and girls of the Hitler Youth Movement, and anyone who wanted to, or had to be seen, paraded through town accompanied by martial music from the fire and police department marching band and the Hitler Youth drum and bugle corps. After nightfall the police department marching band and the Hitler Youth drum and bugle corps led a torchlight parade of Nazi party members through the inner city to the steps of city hall. There the mayor, surrounded by the faithful, gave an inspiring speech praising the Führer's many accomplishments — his rise from poor boy, his service to the Fatherland in the Great War, his struggles during the turbulent times of the "Great Depression" and the attempted "Communist takeover" of the government during the late 1920s and early 1930s, his wonderful vision of a Greater Germany, and now his exceptionally brilliant leadership in the "struggle for Germany's survival against all odds."

In this particular year Reich Youth Leader Arthur Axmann issued a declaration that was to be a show of solidarity for the Führer: All German youths aged ten and above were conscripted into the Hitler Youth Movement. Some confusion, as well as consternation, followed. The mechanism for such drastic action was not in place, but very soon these problems were solved and even in our small corner of Germany we soon attended youth meetings twice each week, Wednesdays and Saturdays from 3 to 5 P.M. Laggards were treated as truants and picked up by the police. As a ten-year-old I and my classmates became members of the German Youth Movement.[4] Those fourteen years or older "volunteered" and joined the Hitler Youth Movement.[5] Uniforms and badges differed, but little else. Initially it was fun. The younger boys received some rudimentary training in close order drill, marched, sang songs, and were steeped in the glories of the Führer and the Nazi party. I soon became bored with marching to the orders of some other kid. Luckily one of my cousins, a very talented musician, was the leader of the local German Youth drum and bugle corps; I was admitted as a drummer and remained in the unit for some time. I received a large kettle drum, four drumsticks — two always in reserve tucked into the loops of the carrying strap — and for the first several months I used every free moment to practice the various drummer drills in our back pasture. Then, every Wednesday afternoon during the mandatory youth meeting, the band practiced together. As soon as I became competent in the art of banging that enormous drum I was allowed to participate in the Saturday afternoon musical presentations on the market square. The Hitler Youth Movement had, as far as I was concerned, a more interesting agenda. They received regular training in small-bore rifle firing; there were special glider pilot units, naval auxiliaries, and horse cavalry units — all in preparation for future military service.

The war continued. It seemed that the occupation of Denmark and Norway was a mere sideshow. On the 10 May 1940 German troops attacked France and the Benelux countries. The Silesians, in the First German Army under General von Witzleben,[6] had one of the most difficult tasks; they charged through the Maginot Line which the French, as well as most others, considered to be impossible to pierce. The Führer wanted to demonstrate to the world that "for a German soldier nothing is impossible." With successive victories this soon became a most popular slogan. During May, June, and July of 1940 the *Jauersches Stadtblatt*, our hometown newspaper, was filled with death notices. Silesia had lost the cream of its youth.

We had not had any letter from Father for some time. Then, in the last week of June, we received the horrible news that he had been severely wounded and had been evacuated to a hospital in the western part of Germany. We learned later that shrapnel had ripped into the right side of his chest. The entry in Father's army records reads:

> 16 JUNE 40: Breakthrough battle of the Maginot Line, south of Saarbrücken.
>
> 17–18 JUNE 40: Attack across the Seille and the Rhine-Marne Canal, 6. Kompanie/461 Infantrie.
>
> 18 JUNE 40: Artillery shrapnel, right chest, 6. Kompanie/461, Schweiseingen, Rhine-Marne Canal.
>
> 18 JUNE 40: Frontline Hospital 3/509.
>
> 18–23 JUNE 40: Aulhausen Hospital.
>
> 24 JUNE 40–10 AUGUST 40: Ehingen Hospital.
>
> 10 AUGUST 40: Urach Hospital.
>
> 10 SEPTEMBER 40: Awarded wounded medal.

As always, Herr Goebbels' propaganda machine was on the move. In May a strange name was mockingly mentioned on the radio and in the papers: Churchill. He was a rather rotund man who wore formal dress and a bowler hat, and smoked large cigars. For some unknown reason he had replaced tall, skinny, and also funny-looking Chamberlain.

Soon, at all carnivals and sideshows, one could win cute little pop-up figurines with bobbing heads that looked surprisingly like Churchill wearing a bowler hat and like Chamberlain with a tall top hat.

In late autumn Father came home on convalescent leave. He proudly displayed his scar and the shrapnel. The shrapnel, about the size of an injector razor blade, only somewhat heavier, had torn through the metal button of his tunic and through his army pay booklet. Then it had ripped into, and twisted its way through, the pocket-sized version of the New Testament and his *Schutzbrief*, a quasi-religious letter of safe conduct that our superstitious Preuss Oma had made all her sons and sons-in-law carry into battle.[7] For years thereafter Preuss Oma insisted that the letter had saved Father's life — and who could argue against her? The doctors said that without the books in his tunic, the shrapnel would have torn through Father's chest and it most certainly would have killed him. However, Father was home and well again. We enjoyed his leave enormously and walked proudly through the old town. Everyone knew that Father had been wounded and was recuperating. He wore his black iron wounded badge proudly. Soon, too soon for us, Father had to return to duty. We walked him to the railroad station. There he presented his papers to the military processing agent, and soon the train carried him away. Because of the severity of his wound he was transferred from the infantry into the Luftwaffe as a crew chief for a heavy antiaircraft gun. He first served in Czechoslovakia, later in Austria and Bavaria.

For a while, with the victory in the West, the war seemed to have come to a standstill. Then, during the harvest season, the Führer once again demonstrated his prowess. We were assured that the Luftwaffe, led by the noble Reichsmarschall Hermann Göring, would beat England into submission. Operation *Adlertag*[8] commenced. First, very wisely, the Luftwaffe attacked airfields and command centers in England. Then, at 5 P.M. on 7 September, 300 German bombers dropped more than 300 tons of bombs on London. The London Blitz had begun. Of course, we knew that the bombing of London was in retaliation for the British bombing of German towns; everyone understood this. Even Grandfather thought the *Britischers* could not resist much longer. Maybe, just maybe, "that fella in Berlin" did know what he was doing. However, Grandfather's doubts about the Führer's infallibility returned soon after Hitler signed an alliance agreement with Italy in late September. Grandfather remembered the Italians from the First World War — they could not be trusted. He thought Hitler, a veteran of that war, should have known better.

"They'll stab him in the back, for sure. Just like they did us in the First War. They can't be trusted. You mark my word!"

But, with the harvest in full swing, Grandfather had more important things to worry about: the weather and hiring new helpers from an ever-shrinking manpower reservoir to replace those drafted into the services. In late summer we celebrated the harvest festival. We attended church services, brought sheaves of rye and wheat, baskets filled with apples, pears, and plums, and large bouquets of flowers to the altar. In sermons priests and ministers thanked the Lord for this year's plentiful offering and prayed that he protect the Führer and our lads on all fronts so they could return home after final victory. We all prayed that the good Lord bestow wisdom and courage upon our Führer and his assistants, as well as the General Staff. Sitting in the private booth next to Grandfather I thought I heard him murmur under his breath, "Dear Lord, especially lots of wisdom for the *Gefreiter*,[9] he needs it most." There were just a few weeks left to finish bringing in the sugar beets before Christmas preparation started. In November my mother started baking our Christmas specialties: *Pfefferkuchen*, *Mohnkuchen*, and *Streuselkuchen*. We were not certain whether Father would be home for the holidays, so preparations were made to mail our Silesian specialties so that he too could celebrate our most important holy days. We dreaded the thought of having to celebrate Christmas without him, but he came home; it was his regularly scheduled leave. Again family men received preference for Christmas leave. This was our second Christmas of the war. We did not know how many more were to follow, but looked forward to the New Year, hoping 1941 would bring us peace.

Opposite: The family photo, taken in late 1940, that survived in Berlin. **Left to right:** Mother, the author, sister Helga, and Father, home on convalescent leave after having been severely wounded during the breakthrough of the Maginot Line in June 1940. *Author's collection.*

Chapter 3

1941

With the new year just starting, and the snow about one to two feet high, we harvested ice for the local breweries. Yes, even in the cold months of winter Grandfather made money. The breweries needed the ice, the Neisse River produced the cleanest and clearest ice in all of Silesia, and he had the horses and sleds to bring the ice to the icehouses. Lacking manpower Grandfather entrusted me to handle one of his teams of horses. The farmhands cut and hoisted ice from the Neisse River onto sleds. Loose straw covered the bottom of the sled. Each slab of ice in turn was covered with straw to facilitate unloading—the straw kept the slabs from freezing together into one unmanageable hunk. I drove the sled to one of the well-insulated, earth-covered cellars not far from the river's bank where the brewers stored the ice.

Soon winter vacation was over and I continued my education at the middle school. Every weekday morning my classmate Lothar Scholz and I left the farm around 7:30 and walked to school along Vorwerkstrasse. I was always eager to leave, hoping to see Ursula Hermann; her friends called her "Uschi." She talked to me once, in the schoolyard, and I had a terrible crush on her. If at all possible I wanted to time it so that I could walk behind Uschi and her girlfriend. Unfortunately, Lothar delayed our exit almost every day by combing his hair incessantly. Several times I almost walked out without him, but we had gone to school as buddies for so long, it was difficult to change. Apparently Lothar had not noticed these two pretty girls—but I had.

For a while the news from the front was sparse, not too much activity. Although Grandfather's suspicions that the Führer was in over his head were confirmed when German troops had to help Hitler's Italian allies who had invaded Albania, Yugoslavia, and Greece the previous year. According to Grandfather, the Italians just could not do anything right. "Here we go again. They can't even beat the Albanians, they can't do anything right. First they surrender at Tobruk to the *Britischers* — well, at least the *Britischers* are fighters! Next thing we'll hear our lads have to go to Africa to pull the Italians' chestnuts out of the fire there. I bet they couldn't even carry water in a bucket — and that *Gefreiter* allies himself with that bunch."

"Uschi." *Author's diary.*

In May 1941 another rather strange thing happened: The much-loved — many women thought he was the most handsome man on earth — Rudolf Hess, the Führer's trusted deputy, flew to England. For the first time in his career Herr Goebbels, our propaganda minister, was speechless. For a few days no one could come up with a good, or at least reasonable, explanation. Then came the announcement: "Hess had suffered a mental breakdown." According to Grandfather, he was not the only one in Berlin. Soon thereafter Hess jokes appeared everywhere; told carefully, and only to trusted friends, they quickly made the rounds:

> Churchill asks Hess, "Are you the crazy one?" "No sir," Hess replies, "I am his deputy."
> An entry at the end of the Royal Air Force Daily Activity

Report reads: "Today no *Reichsminister* has penetrated British airspace."

British press notice: "Today we learned that Hess is indeed insane — he wants to go back to Germany."

Within the family Grandfather's derogatory comments were thought to be rather witty. Certainly, he and his regimental comrades from the Great War thought so. However, even this boy, a member of the German Youth Movement, as well as my older cousin, leader of the German Youth Movement's drum and bugle corps, knew that nothing went beyond Grandfather's living room. Actually we became quite adroit at listening to Grandfather's anti–Hitler remarks on the one hand, and mouthing the Nazi party line at Wednesday and Saturday afternoon youth meetings on the other. However, the whole family worried about Grandfather and his regimental comrades. They met every Saturday at noon at Kaulbach's, the premier restaurant in town. There each of the old-timers tried to tell the newest and most hilarious (and also most incriminating) jokes and stories about the *Gefreiter* and his "helpers-helpers," their name for all Nazi party members. Herr Kaulbach was terribly afraid that "the whole bunch," including himself, "could end up in jail." One Saturday evening, after Grandfather had returned from Kaulbach's, he asked us what a real German should look like. No one knew. Then he told us his latest tidbit: "A real German is blond like Hitler, athletic like Göring, clear-eyed as Himmler, with physical prowess like Goebbels." Everyone thought this was indeed humorous, because Hitler had black hair, Göring was terribly overweight, Himmler was near sighted and squinted through strong glasses, and Goebbels was handicapped with a club foot.

I must admit, as I grew older, the world did seem a bit confusing. It seemed as if May was a month for bad news. The mighty German battleship *Bismarck*, dispatched into the North Atlantic to destroy British shipping, was sunk on the 27th of May. A few days thereafter we heard that Kurt Baumert my Uncle Gerhard's brother-in-law, had perished in that disaster. We all knew Kurt well; he grew up directly across the street from our farm. He was a few years older, far more serious and responsible than the rest of us troublemakers.

During the summer of 1941 we visited our Uncle Willy in Oberseeberg, in Poland. He was the police chief for the area. Oberseeberg was not far from my mother's birthplace, Pinne. We rode the train all day and finally arrived at Oberseeberg. Uncle Willy met us at the railroad station. A few days later Father arrived on army leave. He, my mother, and my sister went by bicycle to see the old Preuss homestead in Pinne. A few days later we went on another trip. This time I went along as we visited one of my mother's cousins who lived on a farm at the Warthe River. The cousin had a horse that laughed on command. While we were eating the horse stuck his head through the dining room window. My mother's cousin shouted a command, and the horse actually laughed. One curious thing, they fed mussels to their ducks. There were piles of shells dredged from the Warthe River. It gave the duck meat a fishy flavor.

There was something odd about Uncle Willy. He had originally been stationed in a small town in northwestern Germany. When the Nazis incorporated Czechoslovakia into Greater Germany Uncle Willy was suddenly transferred from that quaint little place to Czechoslovakia. That in itself was rather unusual, because local police officers remained in their home towns for life. Shortly after Germany had defeated and occupied Poland he was transferred to Oberseeberg, a small town somewhere north of Posen — the area where Mother's family had lived for generations, and where he was born before the turn of the century. Later, in the autumn of 1944 — we learned this after the end of World War Two — Uncle Willy was again removed from his post and assigned to an antipartisan unit in eastern Poland. There, at the start of the Soviet winter offensive, Uncle Willy, who spoke fluent Polish, with several Russian-speaking SS men from the Baltic nations under his command, was overrun by Soviet forces. Their winter uniforms being similar to those of the Soviets, they spent weeks behind Soviet lines driving a *Panje* wagon across Poland. They rode among the advancing Soviets and finally made a hair-raising escape through the Soviet and German lines. Well, it turned out that the Nazis carried a long grudge. Shortly before they took power a farmer complained to Uncle Willy that some local Nazis were practicing close order drill on the farmer's hayfield. As a good police officer Uncle Willy followed up the complaint, went to the hayfield, and asked the leader of the group not to ruin the grass. A confrontation, for which Uncle Willy was partly responsible, resulted in the Nazi leader pushing — or hitting — Uncle Willy. Uncle Willy — formerly a police physical education instructor and police middle-weight boxing champion — hit the Nazi once and broke his jaw. They never forgot! During the intervening years they assigned Uncle Willy to places where he could have been "killed in the line of duty."

In 1941, with many farmhands called into the army, Grandfather entrusted me, now almost a teenager, with driving a team of horses during harvest time. We had several horses including, two large Belgian cold-bloods, of light brown color, the size of Clydesdales. Grandfather named them after two German comic story characters, Max and Moritz. We also had an old mare, Grete, and her daughter, Lotte. You had to treat Lotte with care, she would bite! And then there was my favorite horse, Stutti. She was a chestnut mare of fine breeding, classified by the German Army as a riding and light wagon horse. Stutti was the most affectionate horse I have ever known. Whenever I called her she came galloping across the meadow. There were a few other horses whose names I have forgotten, and we always had two or three colts grazing in the orchards.

With the world in turmoil, life in Jauer was very peaceful; it was so peaceful that it was boring. Only the death notices in our daily newspaper reminded us that friends and neighbors were dying in faraway places. Beyond Jauer's horizon the world was aflame. German troops fought in Yugoslavia, Albania, and Greece. When the *Britischers* threatened to wipe out the Italians in North Africa, German soldiers, this time Field Marshal Rommel's Afrika Korps, came to the rescue. "I told you so," Grandfather rasped, "those Italians can't carry water in a bucket. Wait, they'll stab us in the back yet."

On 20 April we once again celebrated the Führer's birthday. Again, the town's store owners vied for the best window decoration with gorgeous displays of oak leaves, pine boughs, and the large oil painting retrieved from their storage rooms. During the afternoon and evening our drum and bugle corps marched through the streets of town playing for the folks. Alas, this year there seemed to be a shortage of wax candles; after sundown most store fronts were dark. Later, we even gave an evening performance in one of the large dance halls provided for the occasion by a patriotic owner. I enjoyed this because there were only two drummers, I was one of them, and we stood in the front row of the band. That was the first time I had ever performed on a stage — great fun. Even Mother enjoyed that one. However, this year there was no torchlight parade.

Hess had become a nonperson and was soon forgotten. Far more

Opposite: The Protestant *Friedenskirche*, the Church of Peace. *Author's collection.*

serious events became topics of conversation. In June 1941 Hitler committed, according to Grandfather, his worst mistake: He invaded Russia. Early victories made Grandfather wonder as German troops stormed victoriously across the steppes. Then the harsh Russian winter, "General Winter," the Russians called it, stopped our army in its tracks. "The *Gefreiter* hasn't read his history," Grandfather lamented, "Napoleon did the same thing, and see what happened to him!"

On 1 November 1941 Father became an *Obergefreiter* (lance corporal). A month later, on 7 December 1941, the Japanese attacked Pearl Harbor, and Hitler declared war on the United States. The folks in Jauer knew little, and cared less, about Pearl Harbor. They could not understand why Germany had to declare war on America, but the Führer probably knew things to which the simple folks were not privy. They busily prepared for another winter, and for another Christmas — the third one with the world at war.

Christmas was always Jauer's most festive holiday. During the war, with Father home on leave, it just could not be better. We bought a Christmas tree at the *Pferdemarkt*, the horse trader's market, on Neumarktstrasse. We decorated it with delicate Christmas ornaments. On Christmas Eve the warm glow of the wax candles reflected in the snow that gently covered meadows and forests. Ah, how I remember the heavenly smells of Christmas, the aroma of *Pfefferkuchen*, the fresh smell of the pine tree. Toward dusk we listened to the pealing of the bells from the Protestant *Friedenskirche* near our farm, and the resonant clang of the large bells high in the steeple of the Catholic St. Martin *Kirche* with its commanding view from the highest hill in town. The most beautiful snow started falling. First a few fine, dusty flakes, and then, ever increasingly, the snow covered our little town in the foothills of the Sudeten Mountains with the most pristine blanket of white. That was Christmas in Jauer.

I heard Father and Grandfather conversing. Grandfather thought that the *Gefreiter*'s worst mistake was attacking Russia. Father thought Hitler made his fatal mistake declaring war on America. He told Grandfather that Hitler had no idea how strong and big America really was. Grandfather thought the Americans were not as tough as the *Britischers*, but had more money, and "Money makes the world go 'round," he said. Father replied, "This time he overstepped himself." He opined that declaring war on the United States meant the end of Germany as we knew it, and that Germany would lose the war for sure. He told Grandfather that those Nazis just did not know what a great and powerful country the United States was. Grandfather said nothing, he only nodded his head sadly.

Chapter 4

1942

I do not remember anyone who thought that it was a good idea for Germany to declare war on the United States, but of course no one dared to say so—except Father. However, it was not long before the first of Germany's small, 500-ton submarines arrived off the U.S. coast. They raised hell from New York all the way to Key West, Florida. We were proud of our daring lads in the navy. At the same time it surprised us that those small boats could travel so far from home waters and strike such terrible blows without suffering any losses whatsoever. So, many folks thought, maybe the Americans were not so tough after all, and maybe the Greatest Field Marshal of All Times had a view of the world that was superior even to those of his generals and admirals.

Shortly after New Year's 1942 a call went out for all citizens to bring winter clothing, heavy wool socks, woolen underwear, skis, and snowshoes to a central collection point. Our lads at the Eastern Front were in dire need of extra clothing and skis. According to Grandfather, "Apparently the Greatest Field Marshal of All Times had indeed forgotten the lessons of Napoleon's retreat from Moscow." Whatever, the brave folks of Jauer, including Grandfather, contributed because, after all, the Nazis in Berlin were cozily warm in their offices, but our lads on the Eastern Front were freezing. We entered the third year of the war.

The winter of 1941-1942 was a bitter one. To me it seemed as if Germany had been at war forever. With every battle Germany won, the front lines got longer. Soon Germany had conquered almost all of Europe. Jauer's simple folks, the sons of butchers and farmers, farmhands and mechanics, tailors and bakers, scribes and office managers, fought and died in the frigid cold of the Arctic Circle and the searing heat in North

Africa. They looked across the English Channel at the White Cliffs of Dover, and rode tanks through the hot dusty Libyan Desert. Our Uncle Gerhard and many other friends and neighbors marched across the frozen steppes of Russia. Some roamed the oceans in battleships and merchant cruisers. A few patrolled in small submarines under the icy waters of the North Atlantic and beyond South Africa's Capetown into the vast Indian and Pacific oceans — and they died in God-forsaken places no one had ever heard of or could pronounce. This turned out to be a terribly cold winter. Rarely did we venture out after dark during the bitterly cold evenings. This year wolves from the Polish plains roamed the outskirts of town looking for food. Farmers traveled into town and back to their farms only during daylight hours, and even then they kept their shotguns at the ready. Again, we harvested ice from the river for the breweries. Around four in the afternoon, when dusk fell, I came into our warm living room. The *Kachelofen* (tile stove) made it ever so cozy. Mother had tea and cookies ready. I peeled off the wet, frozen trousers and sweaters and untied the frozen shoelaces. Once I was dressed in dry clothing, my sister, Helga, and I sat on the bench with our backs against the warm tiles of the stove. It was heavenly. And, aside from the rationing and the absence of fathers and friends, here in Jauer the war was only a distant uneasiness.

In early spring British troops attempted a landing on the French coast at St. Nazaire but, to everyone's relief, were repelled. However, it was an indication that sooner or later the allied Americans, French, and British forces would attempt just such an invasion. In the meantime our propaganda minister proclaimed joyfully that "Germany was winning on all fronts"— and so were the Japanese. We were just happy that Father was in a relatively safe place in Austria with his antiaircraft gun.

Although it was not terribly important to world events, in 1942 Jauer celebrated its 700th anniversary as a chartered town. Military and fire company bands entertained the citizens. The mayor recounted the proud history of the town. He alluded to the happy amalgamation of our Slavic and Germanic ancestors who had built and defended this town since ancient times and how Jauer would be here for our children and children's children to enjoy — and for a short time the war was forgotten.

We were hard at work throughout the summer. Once again I drove a team of horses, with Stutti my favorite, to bring in the harvest. The vegetable garden kept Mother and my sister busy. It was almost a full-time job. Soon the kitchen was crowded with all the females in the family canning fruits and vegetables. Much that could not be canned was dried; many plums, apples, and pears were washed, sliced, and then placed on drying racks. In late winter the dried fruit was much appreciated. Later yet came the time to make syrup from sugar beets, one of our prime crops. We even brought to Preuss Oma the residue from boiled and pressed sugar beets so that she too could make syrup. The whole house reeked of damp, sweet sugar beets, but in late winter and early spring we enjoyed that dark, sweet syrup on our sandwiches. And then came another Christmas. It was a never-to-be-forgotten festival with Father home on leave for just a few days.

Chapter 5

1943

Ever so slowly the war took a turn for the worse. Since early 1943 I and my classmates had followed news dispatches of "temporary" setbacks with growing concern. Without a doubt the first truly devastating news flash was the encirclement of the Sixth German Army at Stalingrad in November 1942 when Soviet forces had surrounded the 6th Army, and parts of the Fourth *Panzerarmee* (Tank Army). At school we updated our daily activity map and drew the battle lines, blue for the heroic Germans, red for the dreaded enemy. The ring around Stalingrad became ever tighter; the blue area held by General Paulus became ever smaller. After more than two months of desperate fighting we heard the terrible news that true to their oath the soldiers of 6th Army had fought to the last man and the last shell for Germany, and that with the surrender of the German XI Korps all German resistance at Stalingrad had come to an end — and then we erased the blue circle at Stalingrad from our map. The whole country was in mourning, yet we also were proud of our soldiers. They had fought long and hard. Nearly 150,000 Germans had died, 91,000 were captured. Under normal circumstances the ratio of killed and captured should have been reversed, but most of our soldiers had chosen death over capture.[1] This tragedy was followed by other devastating news.

In May 1943 some 250,000 Germans and Italians were captured in North Africa — and we erased all blue entries from our North Africa map. "Haven't I told you," Grandfather proclaimed, "it's those damn Italians. Because of them we now lost the whole Afrika Korps. They should never have been in Africa. We have other, more important fish to fry."

During the summer of 1943 German troops regained some of the lost territories in the east, but with prohibitive losses. In July the battle of Kursk — the greatest tank battle in history and, according to Herr Goebbels, a tremendous German victory — ended with dubious results. German forces under two highly experienced panzer generals, Herman Hoth and Walther Model, equipped with 2,000 of Germany's most modern tanks, including the new Panthers and Tigers, as well as with the highly effective Ferdinand self-propelled gun, attacked from the north and the south along a 200-mile-wide front. The Germans had concentrated 37 division — 17 armored, 2 motorized, and 18 infantry — in the Orel-Kursk and Belgorod sectors. About 5,000 to 6,000 German and Soviet tanks, supported by 4,000 aircraft and 2 million men, clashed. Losses were terrible on both sides. Germany lost 70,000 men, 2,900 tanks, 195 Ferdinand self-propelled guns, 844 guns, 5,000 trucks, and 1,392 aircraft. It was rumored that Field Marshal von Mannstein had ordered the withdrawal despite Hitler's instructions to "stand and fight to the last man." Soon thereafter von Mannstein, one of Germany's most brilliant generals, was retired. For most of 1943 we had heard very little good news. Even Herr Goebbels did not seem to be his usual exuberant self. Even in his periodic declarations that "Germany is winning on all fronts," he did not sound as convincing as in earlier years.

For farmers the summer of '43 was a busy one. With Germany in its fourth year of the war, food supplies were critical. We had some of the wheat knocked down by a sudden rain squall and Herr Baumert came by to help save some of the wheat by cutting the knocked-down portions with the scythe. A raw-boned man who walked with a perpetual stoop from a lifetime of hard labor, he was one of the very few who knew how to cut wheat with the scythe. Tough, yet gentle, his face was graced by a large salt-and-pepper mustache. He lived directly across the street from our estate in an old house on cemetery property; he was a grave digger by profession. This year again, Grandfather asked three of his grandchildren to handle the horses during the harvest. While many of my schoolmates summered on the Baltic Sea or high up in the Sudeten Mountains I did my patriotic duty helping with the harvest. And, once again I was in charge of my two favorite horses, young Stutti and old Grete. Few understood how I could love getting up at 5 A.M. during my summer vacation, working all day for practically nothing — Grandfather was not a generous man — and enjoy it. Well, as a teenager it was difficult to explain, but now, with time to reflect, it is quite simple: At heart I am a romantic — something I never would have admitted in 1943. There was something so beautiful about walking under still dark skies across the farmyard into the warm stables. Calling to the still sleeping horses, having them turn their heads in return greeting — most horses sleep standing up. Then their grateful movements as we fed them. The camaraderie between the horse drivers at first breakfast — coffee, black bread with butter and jam — was just great. Then, with the horizon already getting light, harnessing the horses and riding the wagon into the field to cut alfalfa that fed the dairy cattle. The smell of freshly cut alfalfa, the beautiful melodies of the meadowlarks high in the sky, and then the return to the farm for our second breakfast — we ate three breakfasts. Second breakfast was rich: scrambled eggs, black bread, milk fresh from the stables and still hot from pasteurization. Third breakfast was, again, coffee, black bread with butter and jam. It was a great experience, especially since the adults treated us young horse handlers as equals.

Before summer vacation our teacher had asked us to keep a diary during our vacation for additional credits. Reluctantly I agreed to keep one — I needed the extra credits. My first entry read something like this:

> 8 July 1943
>
> Dear Diary,
>
> I am once again helping with the harvest, and again with my two favorite horses, young Stutti, and old Grete. Our routine is all set: we rise before sunup. After a light first breakfast we are off to the stables to harness the teams. Then we drive into the fields before the morning sun even has a chance to bathe the fields in gold and green. There we cut feed for the dairy cows. The mower cuts a wide swath into the alfalfa. I follow the mower so that the farmhands can load my wagon. These early morning hours are unforgettably beautiful. The meadows are wet with dew. Meadowlarks rise high into the sky reaching for the first rays of the sun and reward the early risers with their melodious songs. Ah, city folks don't know what they are missing! We are back in the farm before seven, feed the horses and eat our second breakfast. Then we clean the stable, harness the horses, and once again it's out into the fields. This time with the large wagons that carry the huge loads of grain-laden straw into the barn for threshing in late Autumn.[2]

For us young horse handlers farm labor was not particularly hard, but we worked long hours driving huge wagons loaded high with bundles of grain straw to be stored in the barns for threshing in early winter. Our upper bodies became dark brown while below the belt we remained pale, because only a fool wore shorts while sitting on and sliding off bales of barley or wheat. The bristle-like beards of these cereals became forever lodged under the skin. At the city swimming pool one could always tell the farmboys from the city slickers: The "townies" had tanned legs. Life in the country was wholesome fun. Only the daily war reports, the war that by 1943 had engulfed Europe and the world, spoiled an otherwise bucolic atmosphere.

Throughout this time Herr Goebbels' propaganda machine continued and, increasingly louder, insisted that victory was just around the corner. Slowly, even the simple folks living far from important events and significant places in the foothills of the Sudeten Mountains started to realize that not everything Herr Goebbels said was entirely true — not everything. Of course, no one dared to say it out loud; that would have been treasonous.

In July 1943 Father transferred to the 6th Battery of the 388th Heavy Antiaircraft Artillery Section at Linz. Just a little later we received a cryptic note from Father that he and his Flak unit were on their way to the Russian front — escorting a supply train. We were terribly worried. Rail travel through Russia was fraught with danger. His heavy Flak guns, mounted on rail cars, gave fire support against attacking aircraft and the ever-threatening Russian partisans. Every afternoon we waited for news from Father, and every afternoon for a whole month Mother would shake her head: no news. Then finally a letter.

> 30 August 1943
>
> Dear Diary,
>
> We are happy again. We just received the news that Father is back in Linz. His Flak guns were mounted on rail cars to give fire support should the train be attacked by aircraft or partisans. He will have much to tell during his next leave. Will he be home for Christmas again? We all hope so!

When we returned to school after summer vacation our teacher collected newspaper clippings and diary entries from the boys. Under his tutelage boys recorded military events on a situation map in our classroom. Most high schools had maintained such a map, always prominently

Schlesische Heimat!!!

1.) Auch wir haben sie verlassen,
unsre Heimat traut und schien.
mußten wie die Bettelkinder
in die weite Ferne ziehn.

2.) Unsere Herzen sind verwundet, und die Augen Tränen schwer,
getrennt sind wir von unseren Lieben
haben keine Heimat mehr.

3) Unsere Kinderhände heben
Tag u. Nacht sich zum Gebet,
Wie es um den Vater und
die liebe Heimat steht.

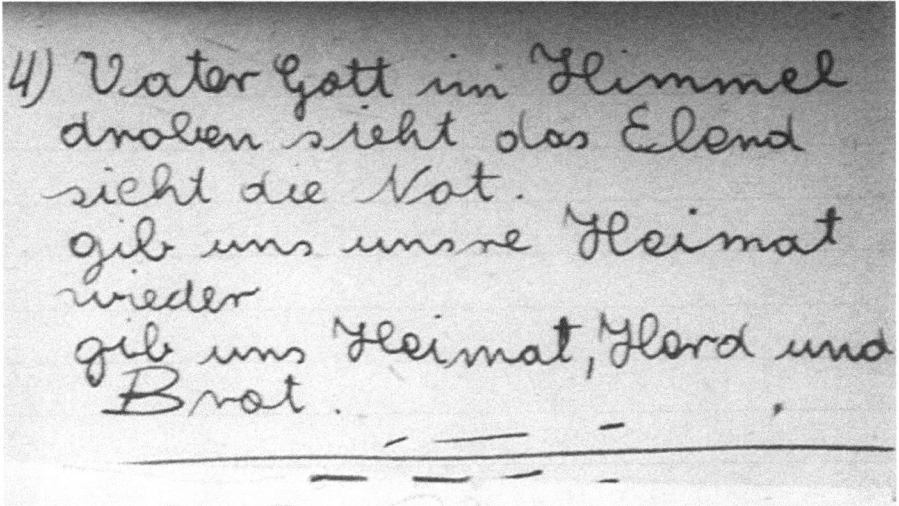

Opposite and top: Silesian homeland. *Author's diary.*

displayed in classrooms, since the beginning of the war. In previous years, when "Germany was winning on all fronts," the front lines had gotten longer and longer until Germany had conquered almost all of Europe and parts of North Africa. In those victorious days the students read letters from neighbors at the start of the school day that told of life in U-boats that roamed the oceans from the North Atlantic to the east coast of the Americas, and past South Africa's Capetown into the Indian Ocean and beyond. For several years my high school class had enthusiastically maintained this map. We had vied for the privilege of marking new battle lines, recording glorious victories. Then it was the fun thing to do. Now, almost at the end of 1943, this was no longer the case. Toward the end of our summer vacation we had learned that Anglo-American forces had attempted an invasion of Sicily. The broadcaster had assured us that the Hermann Göring Division, alongside its Italian allies, was engaged in a bitter battle to throw the enemy back into the sea. Alas, it was not to be. American and British forces captured Sicily in only thirty-nine days and managed to gain a firm foothold in southern Italy two months later. Disgustedly Grandfather said, "Why are we defending Italy? Why can't the Italians defend their own country? I always said my prize horse could make better decisions than that *Gefreiter*."

Father (*center*) with his antiaircraft artillery. *Author's collection.*

Since the Americans and their allies had been steadily gaining ground on the Italian peninsular their bombers had started to penetrate the Reich ever more successfully. Whereas in previous years they had entered the Reich only from the British Isles, now they also came from the south across the Alps. With his antiaircraft battery just across the Danube River from the Linz oil refinery, Father saw combat almost daily.

Few realized that Germany had already gone past the point of no return — that all had already been lost. The news from the Eastern Front had us especially worried. "Shortening the front lines" became a favorite topic of the Nazi propaganda machine. For example, after Germany reportedly had won the great tank battle at Kursk we heard on the radio that our forces had completed shortening the front line in the northern and southern sectors of the Kursk front. All wondered, why shorten the front line when the battle was won? What did all that mean? Grandfather opined that shortening the front lines meant we were losing territory to the Soviets, but most others thought it was just another genius way of winning the war by conserving resources.

Another, somewhat disconcerting happening occurred: Several boys and girls from Berlin, Hamburg, and Hanover came into our classrooms and were introduced as *Ausgebombte*, i.e., victims of terror bombers."[3] Hans, one of the boys in my class, said his mother heard a radio announcement that encouraged her to send him to her sister in Jauer. He also told us that Hermann Göring had changed his name to *Obermaier*. Incredulously we asked, "Why Obermaier?"

"Because of a promise Göring made near the start of the war. In 1939 he said that 'if a single enemy aircraft appeared over Germany my name will be Maier.' Since so many are flying over Germany he changed his name to Obermaier."

We dared not laugh in public.

My Grandfather roared when I told him the story. He could hardly wait for the following Saturday to tell the story to his regimental comrades from the Great War at their weekly gathering in Kaulbach's. They howled, they laughed, they shouted, "Another beer for Herr Obermaier," repeating the story to others until Herr Kaulbach, fearful of repercussions, carefully looked around to make sure no Nazi was in the club, and said, "Gentlemen, Gentlemen, not so loud please, or Herr Obermaier may make you pay for that beer." More rowdy laughter from the old gang of veterans from the Great War.

Our local newspaper wrote that it was everyone's duty to make the newly arriving refugees part of our community because the enemy was ruthlessly conducting terror bombings against the civilian population to break our will to fight.[4] There was wide belief that the Führer would retaliate. Goebbels' propaganda machine tried to convince everyone that these criminal acts against humanity would only strengthen German resistance and the will to fight until final victory was assured. Our teacher, although not an ardent Nazi, thought this to be a reasonable assessment of the situation: "If you burn my house, I am not going to love you," and the boys in my class appreciated his comments. "Final victory" soon became just another propaganda slogan.

Some time later my cousin, the leader of the drum and bugle corps, left to join the Hitler Youth marching band. My cousin was, even for his young age, a talented musician. He played the drums, bugle, fanfare, horn, and flute. He was also a good instructor. The new boy leader had little talent — he played only the snare drum — and was a poor instructor. Soon one, then more boys left the band. I heard that a new unit, a Hitler Youth horse cavalry one, was looking for additional boys. Since I was not old enough to join the Hitler Youth I needed a waiver. Herr Pröst, the instructor, an elderly member of the Nazi party's SA,[5] secured the waiver and I left this rather sad marching band to participate in the love of my life — horseback riding.

In September of 1943 Italy, Germany's closest ally, surrendered to the Anglo-American Allies. I can still hear my Grandfather: "Ha, that's the stab in the back I was telling you about." He repeatedly said the German equivalent of "no guts, no glory."

> 1 September 1943
>
> Dear Diary,
>
> Joining the Hitler Youth horse cavalry was the best thing that has happened to me for a long time. Herr Pröst is a kind man, and a great instructor. We are still getting theoretical instructions on the care and feeding of horses, how to prepare the horse, the saddle, the reins, for riding. It's all very interesting, but I know most of that stuff already. The city boys are learning fast, and I have picked up a few things also. Lothar has also joined the unit. Even though he lived on our farm since he was five years old, he knows little of horses. I heard that even girls from the *Bund Deutscher Mädchen*[6] may be admitted to this unit. Now, we all know that girls can't handle horses as well as boys. This should really be fun.

Chapter 5 — 1943

The memory of the losses at Stalingrad had already faded. Although there were other losses, supposedly unimportant ones, that caused German forces to shorten the front lines, the situation in other localities did not appear too serious. The Balkans were solidly in German hands; to the south the high Alps protected Germany's southern frontier, and the impenetrable Atlantic Wall guarded the channel coast from any possible Anglo-American invasion. During the summer of 1943 even on the Eastern Front German troops had regained some of the territories lost during the past winter, alas, though, with huge losses.

Some time ago our homeroom teacher had mentioned that victory was in German hands when our forces on the Eastern Front had crossed the Dniepr River. In October 1943 we heard that Soviet armies of the Central Front, Steppe Front, and Southwest Front were exerting intense pressure on our Army Group Center and Army Group South along the great bend of the Dniepr. We worried when during heavy fighting the Soviets succeeded in crossing the river and establishing small bridgeheads near Kiev, Kremenchug, and Dnepropetrovsk. To our great relief our lads, in rigorous counterattacks, regained some of the lost territory — although Herr Goebbels never said whether all the lost territory was recaptured.

I listened to those who thought that Germany could still be victorious, and to Grandfather and his acquaintances who saw dark clouds on the horizon — harbingers of disaster for the Fatherland. Still, the morale among "grass roots" Germans was high, no matter if it seemed that the whole world was upside down. As the war continued with all its fervor, some events were extremely difficult to fathom. For example, Fascist Italy's surrender alone was difficult to understand since Il Duce and Der Führer, as well as the entire Italian and German governments, were so closely allied. Totally incomprehensible was Italy's next move: In October Italy, the country whose chestnuts Germany had pulled out of the fire at least twice, once in the Balkans and again in North Africa, turned and declared war on Germany. "That goddamned *Gefreiter*," Grandfather lamented, "should have known from the Great War. You can't trust these goddamned Italians. They turn on you the moment something goes wrong." How right he was! But then he added, "Ach, those Italians hadn't done much fighting anyway. Our lads will hold their own without those cowards." We hoped he was right on that one, too. It seemed that Germany had no choice but to occupy Rome to secure lines of communication between the Fatherland and forces on the Italian Front.

15 October 1943

Dear Diary,

Well, just as Herr Pröst had promised, today was our first day at the military riding hall of our garrison. We were introduced to our horses — 20 in all — by the sergeant in charge of the stables. Guess what, three girls have joined our group. They aced the theoretical tests two weeks ago, but today they did not look too good. But then neither did most of the boys. Only the kid from the horse butcher shop and I even knew how to mount a horse. The others flopped all over the place. The butcher boy and I laughed, but Herr Pröst sternly admonished us. So, we just snickered behind his back.

Another incomprehensible event: Germany occupied Hungary and Rumania while Hungarian and Rumanian army units were still fighting bravely alongside their German comrades. Following radio reports with increasing alarm, I heard about American and British troops slowly gaining ground in heavy fighting up the Italian boot. In autumn the German Army's advance all along the Eastern Front came to an abrupt halt. Later fiercely attacking Soviets caused the Germans once more to retreat, and by December of 1943 the Soviets had recaptured much of their territories. "We are only shortening the front lines," Herr Goebbels assured us. And Grandfather mumbled, "Another stoke of genius by the Greatest Field Marshal of All Times."

Slowly my classmates neglected the map. Eventually, and to everyone's relief, the teacher moved it from the highly visible place in front of the classroom to a discreet corner in the back storage room. Outside of school, never one of my favorite activities, I thoroughly enjoyed our riding lessons. We had several great Sunday mornings at the riding hall. The training was getting tougher. The second Sunday Herr Pröst had only three horses in the hall. We placed an eighty-centimeter brush hurdle in the middle of the hall. Then Herr Pröst demonstrated the proper way of falling off a horse.

30 October 1943

Dear Diary

We had fun at the riding hall. Herr Pröst said he would teach us how to properly fall off a horse. First we thought he was kidding, but he explained that the proper way of falling off a horse could mean the difference between injury and walking away. For this exercise the horses had no saddle, only a girth belt with two handles. Then we all learned how to fall from the horse as it cleared the brush hurdle. Actually, after a few practice runs, it was almost fun. The girls had a bit of a problem. I think one of them will not be back next Sunday.

School continued, although now already retired teachers were recalled to take the place of those drafted. Something new for our school system happened: Our new English teacher was a young woman. She was the daughter of a local coal dealer — and she was beautiful. Suddenly all the boys studied English energetically. Her teaching method was also totally different from that of rotund, stern Herr Grünberg, who had been drafted; she corrected our mispronunciation with a smile, not a scowl.

> 5 November 1943
>
> Dear Diary
>
> The situation map remains in the back storeroom. I searched it for the strange-sounding names of towns that appear in daily dispatches: Gomel, Kiev, Zhitomir, and Vitebsk; each name brought news of terrible fighting and of heavy losses.

The folks in Jauer listened with heavy hearts to the news from the battlefields, but it was almost as if we lived on another planet; life in this idyllic town continued undisturbed. As always, only the death notices in our local newspaper reminded us that a terrible war continued unabated. We continued to cultivate our gardens and fields; we harvested our crops just as our ancestors had for centuries. Preuss Oma attended her weekly religious meetings in the *Pfarrhaus*, the minister's office, near the *Friedenskirche*, our Evangelical church. On weekends my Uncle Arthur and Aunt Kläre came from the country into town in horse-drawn wagons. They brought good country butter and bread — totally disregarding the strict rationing laws — and visited and exchanged the latest gossip.

We celebrated another Christmas, the fifth wartime Christmas. A knee-deep powdery blanket of snow covered the earth. Father returned to his unit shortly after Christmas, but a certain homey security blanket of peace and tranquility remained long after he had departed. Aside from the strict rations for food and clothing our corner of the world was calm.

Chapter 6

1944

Nineteen forty-four started like all the other years. Toward the end of 1943 there were a few air raid alarms, but no enemy aircraft penetrated into County Jauer. Grandfather was sure the Allies did not have Jauer on their target maps. The air raid warnings were only a minor irritant. In the eerie hours of the late night the siren on the city hall steeple sounded its terribly penetrating wail. Everyone, wrapped in heavy blankets, hurried into the old kitchen. Lothar Scholz and I eased away from the women and children and opened the back door of the residence. There, toward the east, far beyond the horizon, we sometimes glimpsed for a moment the cold, blue-white fingers of distant searchlights silently caressing the winter sky over Breslau, the provincial capital.

> 5 January 1944
>
> Dear Diary,
>
> Boy, I can hardly wait to go back to school. Learning English from that new teacher is fun. Unfortunately, the news from the fronts is not good. The Americans and British are slowly advancing up the Italian boot, and the Soviets have made significant gains in the east. As if things were not bad enough on the Eastern Front, we just heard the sad news: on 26 December 1943, in the icy waters off the Cape of Norway, the battle cruiser *Scharnhorst* sank fighting single-handedly against a British battle group; 1,884 men lost their lives.

In one memorable speech Joseph Goebbels, the minister of propaganda, declared that effective immediately Germany was in a "state of total war." We did not quite know what that meant, but the phrase "total war" became a slogan and an excuse for the absence of any amenities still requested. For example, there was to be no public dancing in hotels and clubs; punishment for ration card violations became even stricter; breaking-and-entering "under conditions using the blackout" became a capital offense; and casting any public doubts on Germany's victorious conclusion of the war became an offense called "undermining Germany's will to fight." In Berlin early morning horseback riding, thought to be an affront to the working people, was forbidden; some of the most luxurious restaurants were closed as a sacrifice to "total war"; and confectionery stores were turned into grocery stores for the "convenience of the working people." However, concerts, motion picture shows, theatrical performances, and other cultural as well as political events continued unabated. These were believed to be "essential to the well-being of the German people and to the strengthening of the resolve to bring the war to its final and victorious conclusion." As time went on many of Berlin's dictates were ignored. Public and private dance events were popular and large crowds attended on most weekends — especially in garrison towns like ours. Young soldiers wanted to meet girls, young girls wanted to meet young defenders of the Fatherland.

> 30 January 1944
>
> Dear Diary,
>
> This has been some winter. There are almost hourly air raid warnings on the radio. We now can follow on our map the track enemy bombers are taking entering and leaving Germany. We have had a few alarms, but nothing else happened. The alarms are sounded when enemy aircraft come near our area. According to Grandfather no airoplane, that's what he calls these terror bombers, could find Jauer at night.

We had some tough training in our riding classes. Standing in the saddle, jumping over the horse's head, etc., to gain confidence, but most important was endurance training. That meant, according to Herr Pröst, "developing a rider's ass," a leathery hind end. After a long time in the saddle we walked the horses back into the stables. A few weeks ago Herr Pröst started something new. Returning to the stable we saw twenty buckets of cold water — not for the horses, for us. Herr Pröst made all of us drop our trousers, yes, the girls too, and dip our hind ends into the cold water. He said it would be done after every long ride for the next four weeks. I thought it worked. We have had few saddle sores lately.

In 1944 we once again celebrated the Führer's birthday on the 20th of April. The usual parades, but again fewer torches because of further blackout restrictions. The mayor and local Nazi party leaders gave inspiring speeches praising the Führer as the Greatest Field Marshal of All Times. Collectively, we assured the Führer of our undying love and devotion. Grandfather never attended. He reluctantly hung the German flag from the attic window as his only outward show of solidarity, not with the Führer, but with the German people, and especially the lads at the front.

In early 1944 my classmate Lothar finally discovered girls. He, the one who previously made me wait until the last minute to depart for school, practically shot out of the house in the morning. No longer did I have to cool my heels waiting for his departure. I soon found out why: He was timing his departure so that he could walk behind "my" Uschi and her girlfriend. As always, they were early risers and Lothar practically leaped out of his apartment eager to go to school. Suddenly he thought of himself as the greatest catch for any girl, and he fancied Uschi, the one with well-formed legs. It seemed that Uschi was totally oblivious to Lothar's existence. In conversations between schoolmates Lothar often alluded to meeting the "leggy one" after school at one of the downtown cafes. No one believed him, especially since Lothar, Susi, and I did our homework after school either in their upstairs apartment or in our downstairs dining/bedroom apartment. However, nothing deterred Lothar; he spun tales of romantic involvement first with the leggy one, and later he talked about an involvement with one of the waitresses at the cafe. Most wondered aloud about certain inconsistencies. For example, several of the rendezvous at the cafe happened when it was not open for business. But his stories continued, getting ever better with time. We loved listening to his tales, queried him, tried every which way to trip him up, but nothing deterred him.

Although the situation on all fronts appeared to worsen one rarely heard any mention of an impending Armageddon. In one of his ever less frequent speeches to "my German people" during the latter part of the war the Führer appeared to hint that there might just be the slightest of possibilities that Germany could lose the war when he raved, "And should Germany lose this gigantic struggle for its existence, then the goddess of war shall be a whore for money." It was quite an occasion. I had never heard the word "whore" mentioned in polite society, and even then only in discreet whispers.

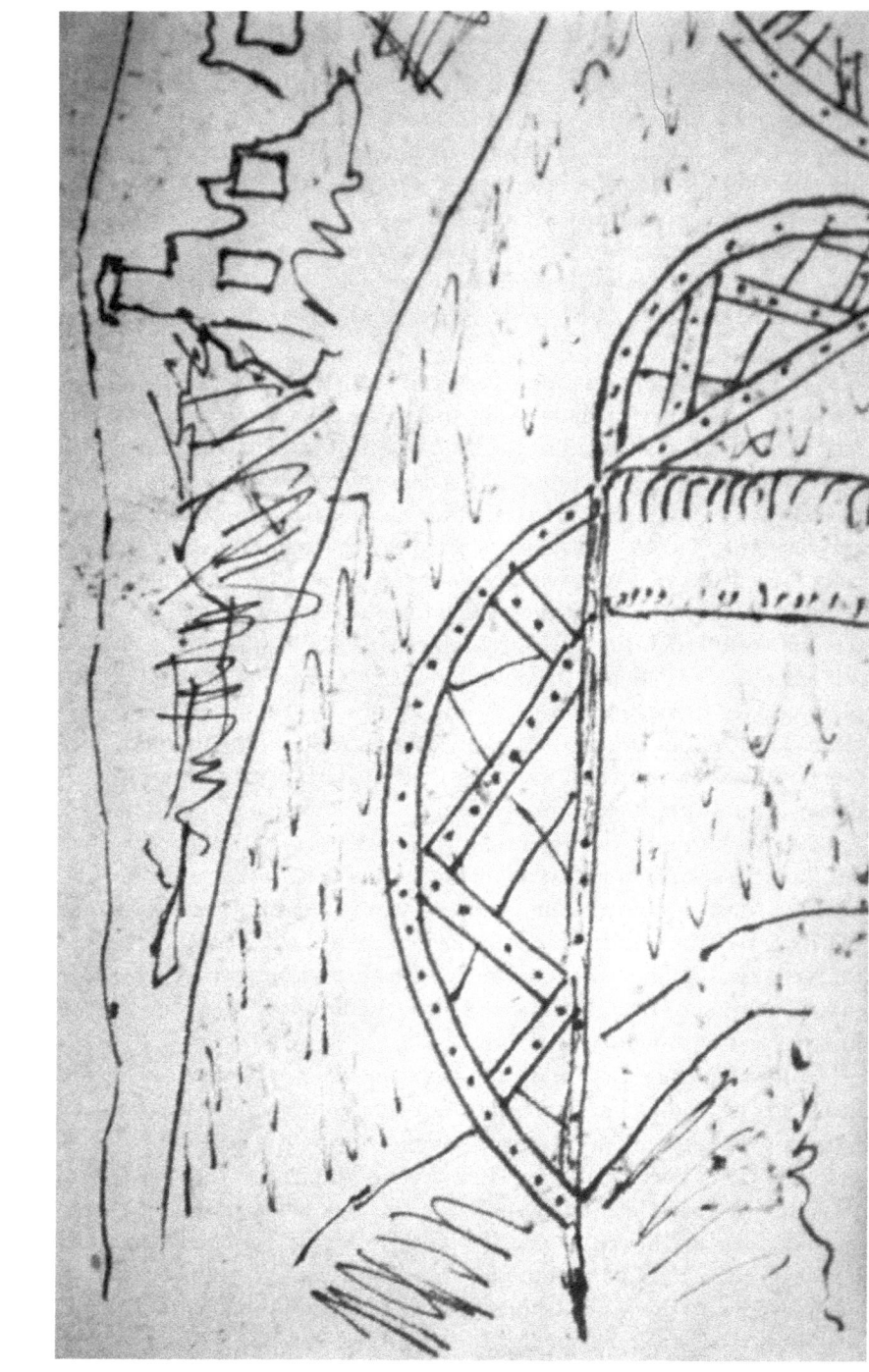

Chapter 6 — 1944

In an announcement on 4 June 1944 Herr Goebbels once again demonstrated to the world Germany's respect for culture and history when he announced that Rome was declared an "open city" to save its cultural structures. At the same time Herr Goebbels brought to the world's attention Anglo-American disrespect for these cultural structures by those countries entering Rome in violation of international law. Grandfather's assessment would probably have been, "Hell, that means we lost another city to the Allies."

News from the Western Front suddenly overshadowed all broadcasts from all other fronts:

> Achtung, achtung, Das Oberkommando
> der Wehrmacht gibt bekannt.[1]
> 6 June 1944. Special Report: The long-awaited attack by British and North American forces against the northern French coast commenced last night.... The battle against the invasion forces is proceeding.[2]

Although American and British forces had landed on the Atlantic coast of France attempting to penetrate the Atlantic Wall,[3] we were assured that the enemy had underestimated our will to fight and that our lads under the command of Field Marshal Rommel, of Desert Fox fame, would shortly push the aggressors back into the sea.

> 19 July 1944
>
> Dear Diary,
>
> There was little doubt that with Field Marshal Rommel in charge of the defense the enemy would indeed be destroyed, possibly even decisively, thus, assuring the Reich's final victory. We are again busy with the harvest. Local Hitler Youth are called up to help with bringing in the crops. I sort of enjoy driving my team, Stutti and Grete, while those city slickers are raking, bundling, and loading the wheat and rye onto my wagon. They know nothing of farm work — and it is killing them. This year they are not vacationing at the Baltic or in the mountains. After all, now we have "total war," and they have to contribute to the war effort. I must admit: they are getting great tans, but only above the waist, just like me.

Opposite: Steel girder bridge destroyed. ***Author's diary.***

For a few days reports from the Western Front told of heavy fighting, then an admission that the task of "throwing the enemy back into the sea" could not be accomplished as quickly as promised. Apparently the Allies had managed to pierce the unpierceable Atlantic Wall.

> Achtung, achtung, Das Oberkommando der Wehrmacht gibt bekannt.
> 9 June 1944. Along the Normandy coast the enemy was able to reinforce its bridgeheads."[4]

In the middle of June the Anglo-American bridgehead had become a sector of the front. Reports from this front told of heavy losses inflicted on the enemy by hard-fighting German forces. Those of us adroit enough to follow the battle on the Western Front on maps soon saw that no matter what losses we inflicted on the enemy, our lads were not exactly winning the battles—the Anglo-Americans were. Indicative of things not going well on the Western Front were the official announcements from that front; they had suddenly received priority over those from the Eastern Front.

In late July 1944 news of a far more serious matter, and totally confusing to most, was announced. A small clique of unscrupulous officers had attempted to assassinate the Führer and the staff of his Supreme Command. Reportedly, a highly decorated army officer had planted an explosive in the Führer's bunker. "Divine intervention" had saved the Führer, although some officers were killed and others severely wounded. Through the immediate actions of loyal officers and men the traitorous clique was eliminated or arrested within a few hours.

Shock, pure shock, throughout the community. In years past we had heard rumors of plots against the Führer, and there had been such an attempt years ago the *Bürgerbräukeller*, at an old Nazi beer joint, a Nazi gathering place before they came to power, in Munich, from which the Führer had miraculously escaped. Nevertheless, it shook the very foundations of Silesian society because the attempted assassination on 20 July 1944 was orchestrated by a group of highly respected German officers and Prussian noblemen, many from Silesia's County Kreisau, our friends and neighbors.

Throughout the land Catholic priests and Protestant ministers thanked God for having protected "the savior of Germany, our leader, Adolf Hitler, from harm so that he may lead our country to final victory." In public meetings everywhere Nazi party leaders loudly proclaimed their undying love and loyalty to the Führer. Military leaders eagerly joined party officials in proclaiming their desire "to fight in defense of the Führer until death."

These events not only confused this teenager, but many adults, even Grandfather, were equally baffled. Since the days of Frederick the Great loyalty to the Fatherland and the finest military training had been the hallmark of the German Army, and for more than two centuries Prussian nobility had supplied the core of its officers. And now? I remembered how proud I was that September morning in 1939 when Father reported for active duty. I remembered so well Father's swearing-in ceremony in 1939, the day he became a German soldier. I remembered the reverent feeling when the officer's saber flashed in the sunlight, and when Father and all his comrades solemnly swore to fight to their death for Führer, *Volk*, and Fatherland. Had all of this been nothing but a charade? Had it meant nothing? Or was there a deeper meaning to the betrayal of the leader of the German people? Why did the very breed of Prussian nobility that had laid the foundation for this great army come to that excruciatingly difficult decision to try to kill the person to whom they had sworn unconditional obedience? In church services across Germany Catholics and Protestants thanked the Good Lord for having saved the Führer, and prayed that his wounds would heal so that he could lead Germany to final victory. Our highly respected minister joined others in praying for God's help so that the Führer could lead Germany to the *Endsieg*, to final victory. He asked God's forgiveness for the heinous act that this small, misguided group of Prussian noblemen from the *Kreisauer Kreis* had committed.[5] Even Grandfather was shocked by this event. Could these men from the neighboring county be so wrong? People were confused; they wondered, *Why would they try to kill the Führer?*

The Kreisauer Kreis conspirators were the most unlikely group to attempt homicide. Field marshals, generals, the former lord mayor of Leipzig, the chief of military intelligence, diplomats, lawyers, philosophers, and labor leaders make poor assassins. They had drawn up elaborate plans for the assassination, as well as for the destruction of the Nazi party, the arrest of all SS[6] units — both the uniformed civilian variety as well as the armed forces elements — and Gestapo[7] members, the take-over of the government, and finally the peace negotiations. Young men with rich, wonderful lives to live had volunteered to blow themselves and Hitler to kingdom come. Others would have to live alone with their consciences: They had caused death or injury to unwitting friends, academy classmates, and respected superior officers while trying to rid the world of a great evil.

With every failed attempt on his life, Hitler's mystique grew. Priests and ministers exhorted their faithful to ask God to preserve and protect "our German savior." Many Germans believed that it was "providence" — that God was on our side, that with God's help the Führer would lead us to final victory. Nazi propaganda broadened this mystique and made Hitler indeed the Greatest Field Marshal of All Times.

Soon the news of internal strife was once again overshadowed by further territorial losses at the various fronts as well as desertions by once highly thought of allies. In August the Allies captured Paris, and

> Achtung achtung. Das Oberkommando
> der Wehrmacht gibt bekannt.
> North American bombers attacked several localities in Upper Silesia.[8]

This news even surprised Grandfather. He had not realized that bombers could fly this far. Was there a possibility that we too could be attacked by these so-called "terror bombers?"

A rather sad event occurred in September: Finland, Germany's finest and most heroic ally, was forced to cease its battle against the Soviets. With Finland out of the war the Fatherland now was left alone to combat the Red Menace. Now the Soviets could concentrate all their forces against our already outnumbered troops. In the Baltic a considerable number of German units were cut off and surrounded. Although surrounded, they continued their battle against the Soviet onslaught and successfully tied down strong enemy elements. A valiant German Navy effort to resupply these elements and evacuate the wounded continued until the very last day of the war. On the southern sector of the Eastern Front the Soviets advanced steadily through Bulgaria, Rumania, and Hungary. On the 5th of September 1944 Bulgaria capitulated.

The world around us was in flames. Enemy aircraft, the "terror bombers," attacked civilian targets indiscriminantly. Yet, on warm evenings, when we rode our horses into the river to wash and to play, war seemed far removed. It is funny how differently each horse entered the water. Some could not wait to splash and roll in the shallows, others had to be backed into the river. Then, once their legs were wet, they splashed like little children. Stutti, my favorite, would first sniff the water and then enter gingerly, first one hoof, then the others. She would find a spot with soft bottom sand. There I would slide off her back into the water and sponge first her neck, then her head, and last her back and legs. Once she was thoroughly soaked, she splashed her belly with strong strokes of her left front hoof. Some horses would lie down and roll in the water, but not Stutti, it was far too undignified for her.

Another announcement hit us like a bombshell: Field Marshal Erwin Rommel had died of wounds received earlier. He was buried deservedly with all military honors.[9] With our most beloved and aggressive *Panzergeneral* gone, who would lead the troops fighting the Allies on the Western Front? Although we did not know Rommel personally, we had heard vivid descriptions of his daring exploits in France and in North Africa; we admired him greatly. He embodied what all thought to be the typical German officer: daring in his exploits, caring for his subordinates, honest with his superiors, fair to his enemies, and loyal to the Fatherland. There were others, but we knew Rommel best. The Fatherland would surely miss him.

> 16 September 1944
>
> Dear Diary,
>
> It was a terrible shock. We just heard on the radio that Soviet forces have entered German territory at Gumbinnen and Goldap in East Prussia. Until now there had only been Russian and Polish town names in the news — now, for the first time since the First World War, Russian troops have captured German towns.

Counterattacking German troops at Rössel County discovered at least 524 civilians murdered by the Soviets. At Kronau, in County Lötzen the Soviets murdered 52 persons, including 18 French prisoners of war. In Nemmersdorf they found 60 women, including a number of nuns, and in Schulzenwalde they found 90 women, who were repeatedly raped and then bayoneted or shot.

Horrible news, but still, East Prussia was far to the north and the east of Jauer. In September 1944 the last cut of hay had to be harvested from the meadow in the Wütende Neisse River valley. Russian armies did not worry farmers; our concern was threatening rains that would ruin the hay. Our luck held out. The powder-dry hay was quickly loaded onto wagons, brought to the cobblestone farmyard, and quickly pitched into the loft above the horse stable. It was another good year and the loft was filled to capacity. In past years my cousins had helped with the harvest, now all had been drafted into the army along with the last able-bodied farmhand. Women and boys had to do even the most difficult tasks. The grain straw was already in the barns for later threshing. The last hay was stored in the hayloft above the horse stables.

    Summer had passed with unbelievable speed. It was time to go back to school, time to pick apples in the orchards that bordered the western and northern sides of the barns and stables, and time to do the never-ending homework. It seemed as if each teacher in our fourth year of middle school thought all the other teachers did not give any homework at all. Demands for reading and writing essays, conducting extensive mathematical calculations, and studying foreign languages left little time for play. Lothar, I, and Susi huddled together to complete the tasks. We did not consider it cheating, more like cooperating. With homework too extensive, we divided the lessons, completed our individual tasks, and then copied each other's work. That at least left us with some free time. Our trio did most of the work in our downstairs living/dining room, on the table under the large lampshade Father had cut from thin plywood. Each panel depicted a scene from "Snow White and the Seven Dwarfs." In late summer of 1944 Mother had been conscripted to work every afternoon at a former farm machinery plant — now converted to casting mortar shells. Mother was already at work when I returned from school. A warm dish was in the oven. After lunch Lothar and Susi came downstairs where we divided our tasks and tackled the homework. We thought we had a pretty slick operation.

    Autumn arrived. In the early morning hours the first cold breaths whitened the pasture. It was time to harvest the "money crop"—sugar beets. As a courtesy to the farming community classes were suspended for three weeks. Conscripted city boys and girls, under the auspices of the Hitler Youth Movement, helped us bring in the harvest. It was hard work, especially for those not used to manual labor. Their hands became raw from pulling beets from piles collected earlier. Some used the wide loading forks Grandfather had provided, but for most it seemed easier to throw the beets on the wagon by hand. From midmorning until late into the afternoon I drove one of the wagons that hauled the money crop to the refinery. The day's last trip from the refinery was the most memorable. I sat comfortably atop the still hot "*Schnitzel*," the remains of the sugar beets. I was surrounded by a wonderfully sweet smell of the still hot shredded remains of the beets that later became silage — winter fodder for the cows. Dusk had slowly engulfed the trees lining the country road. The day's last trip was terribly romantic. I had two strong horses, Stutti and old Grete, pulling the heavy wagon. The wagon's flickering kerosene lanterns cast their dim, yellow light, the air got crisper by the minute, and the horses were eager to return to the stables; they too knew it was the day's last run. I thought, *Can life get any better? How lucky I am! Can the townies ever imagine how wonderful life is on the farm?*

With the sugar beet harvest barely completed all boys fifteen years or older at middle and high schools were ordered to report to the railroad station with camping gear and enough clothing to last two weeks. At the station each was issued a shovel, spade, or pick. The Nazi party organized an appreciation rally for the departing youths. A party leader, along with many other brownshirts, all looking very official in their long coats and jackboots, took charge of the departees; they too carried shovels or spades. With great fanfare all were told that the entire youth of Silesia would build a defensive wall of immense proportions to stop any possible Soviet advance into the Reich.

Plans called for a deep antitank trench that would reach from the eastern foothills of the Sudeten Mountains to the Baltic Sea. The next day our class was somewhat smaller. Lothar was among the ones selected. He was very proud to do his part for the defense of the country. Before he left he confided that this would certainly enhance his position with all the girls in the class. I was not sure the girls even realized he left. I was just sorry he could no longer help with the homework. While he and some of my classmates were digging the great antitank trench the remainder of the class continued its lessons. Homework was levied with the usual heavy volume. Susi, in the other class, and I would now have to shoulder the homework by ourselves — and there was something else.

> October, 1944
>
> Dear Diary,
>
> I am not even sure whether I should write this down, and I still do not know exactly when it happened, but one afternoon, while Susi and I sat at the table doing homework I realized that the top three buttons of her blouse were undone. I was quite certain her blouse was buttoned when we first sat down to do our homework. For the first time I realized that the girl I had known since she was three years old had womanly

breasts—quite endearing, I might add. She acted as if she had not noticed her partially exposed breasts. I could not understand the sudden switch from innocent childhood friends to this new situation, but I found it quite enjoyable. I felt my face flush with embarrassment—it must have turned purple! I found it impossible to divert my eyes from these wonderful features—and Susi seemed to enjoy my uneasiness. I realized that Susi was just as sexy (or maybe even more so) than leggy Uschi. Unbelievable! Utterly unbelievable!!!

At the same time, just after the sugar beet harvest, the senior class had volunteered to produce a comedy scheduled for presentation two weeks before Christmas. The boys of the senior class were given extraordinary permission to meet with the girls of that class in the school auditorium. Uschi, was there as well as her girlfriend. Three of the boys and one girl had written a rather humorous play that had a policeman doing all sorts of silly things that were to come back to haunt him toward the end of the play. I was the policeman; it involved Uschi and her girlfriend. After each practice session our trio walked part of the way home together. With the quickly developing natural familiarity stories were passed back and forth. Conversation centered mostly on various relationships between girls and boys. I spoke only in generalities, never mentioning my newly found relationship with Susi.

October 1944

Dear Diary,

Just as I had always suspected, neither Uschi nor her girlfriend had ever been to the cafe of Lothar's famous rendezvous. I told them about Lothar's adventures, and we all had a good laugh. So much for romantic interludes. It also seems as if I no longer have much interest in either leggy Uschi or her girlfriend.

While we were at play, the Americans and their allies made great advances into Germany proper. There was a report that the famous city of Aachen had been captured, and the Allies were making small gains in Italy as well. The good news was that the Soviets seemed to have been slowed down somewhat. Maybe there was still hope, maybe not of victory, but of some kind of peace. In the meantime, homework could not be ignored. With Lothar on the eastern frontier doing his bit for the

Fatherland, Susi and I were entrenched in homework and our newly discovered endearing situation. Time seemed to fly. We worked diligently every afternoon for two to three hours. Teamwork easily reduced a four-hour task by at least a third. However, with the setting of the late autumn sun there rarely was time for outdoor activity after we had completed our task, and our newly discovered indoor activity was terribly interesting. We hoped that no one would notice any change in our behavior; outwardly, among the others, we tried to behave normally. Hopefully, folks were too preoccupied with their daily activities to notice our surreptitious glances. Since Susi had allowed me to discover her breasts, for some reason other girls no longer seemed to be important. It seemed to me that although both Uschi and her girlfriend had grown into pretty sexy-looking girls, Susi was even prettier. But, Susi and I now had another problem: Lothar would soon return from digging the antitank trench, and neither Susi nor I knew how to handle our relationship; no one would have understood. However, our concerns were unfounded. Although Lothar's return from the big trench digging put our romantic interlude on hold, he was too occupied with stories about the big trench.

> October 1944
>
> Dear Diary,
>
> While Lothar told us in excruciating detail about the trench diggers, Susi stood embarrassingly close to me — it made me blush. Luckily, Lothar was too busy with his story to notice. Susi did not help the situation by pinching me occasionally. I was ready to die. Lothar also mentioned that he was going to meet leggy Uschi and her girlfriend near the Rathaus restaurant; I just smiled when I heard about Lothar's exploits.

There was a full school day of show-and-tell from the boys who had returned from digging the big trench. From all accounts, they had a lot of fun working together with many conscripted old men and some women. They told about the "good army chow" they ate, and of chocolate and cigarette rations (five cigarettes per person per day). The teacher asked, "why would we, with our soldiers holding back the Soviets at the eastern border of Poland, dig an antitank trench along the Oder River miles west of Poland's western border?"

No one had an answer. The dire implication of the trench had never occurred to any of us until our teacher brought it up. Then we all wondered, *Why dig a trench along the Oder River? Did the government expect the Soviets to come that close?* What a horrible thought. But surely, and according to the diggers, the Soviets will never be able to cross the Oder River and the big trench.

The news, at least the bad news, was soon evenly divided between the fronts. The radio announced that the American forces had captured Saarlautern — of course with overwhelming forces. I remembered Saarlautern. Father was severely wounded near that town in 1940. That was a little over four years ago when "Germany was winning on all fronts." Now the enemy is closing from the east, the south, and the west. It seems only the north is still in safe hands, although northern Germany too is threatened — those folks up there are under constant enemy attack from the air. During the day large formations of American bombers devastate the cities and during the night British bombers harangue the countryside.

The situation between Susi and me eventually solved itself. At the start of the pre–Christmas recess Susi and her mother boarded the train to visit relatives in a small town in the Sudeten Mountains near the border crossing into Czechoslovakia. I thought it was somewhat unusual that Susi's mother picked this time of year to visit relatives in the mountains. The weather up there is much worse than down here in the lowlands. I wondered, but Lothar, who helped with the last of the sugar beet harvest, thought it not at all unusual. He appeared to have no idea of what had been happening between Susi and me, partly because he was too occupied with stories about leggy Uschi.

Soon it was Christmas, the sixth of the war. Another year of the war came to an end. Susi and her mother had returned in preparation for the holidays. We used judiciously the rare moments we had without either Lothar or one of the other relatives. We hoped that after the holidays our situation would improve, but had little hope that it would. It complicated our living in the same house considerably.

Silesians, evenly divided between Catholics and Protestants, and a deeply religious lot, enjoyed the preparation and celebration of Christian holidays. It was all here: the aroma of *Pfefferkuchen* mixed with the fresh smell of pine trees, the decorations, the warm glow of wax candles. Mother had cooked the traditional Christmas Eve dinner of *Jauersche Bratwürstel, Klössel,* homemade sauerkraut, and the famous *Polnische Sosse*— Polish gravy made of a base gravy to which were added leftover

Pfefferkuchen, several bottles of dark beer, raisins, raspberry syrup, and the juice of a long-hoarded lemon. Oh, it was heavenly. That dinner was served but once each year, and to Silesians it meant that Christmas Eve had finally arrived. As the wonderful aromas of that dinner wafted through the house the little children waited for Santa Claus. But I wondered, *Would there be another Christmas, ever?* Although the dark clouds of Germany's *Götterdämmerung* had already gathered eastward beyond the horizon, Father received a short holiday furlough. The Wehrmacht still took good care of its men. Christmas just could not have been better, although most Silesians celebrated Christmas 1944 with dark thoughts of the future. Soon, too soon for us, Father returned to his antiaircraft artillery unit in Austria.

What would the New Year bring? We heard nothing but bad news from the fronts. At year's end Soviet forces stood a mere 75 miles from the old Polish-Russian border. Through many centuries the folks of Jauer had endured and survived. My German and Polish ancestors had lived through many centuries of strife; would we live through 1945? We celebrated our *Sylvester Abend*—New Year's Eve—with hot cider and by pouring melted lead into cold water to see what the forms would predict for the future. It seemed as if this year the lead emerged from the cold water as twisted forms that in Preuss Oma's peasant logic was an omen of terrible events for the next year. I think we knew that 1945 would not be a happy year. Little did we imagine how horrible reality could be.

Chapter 7

1945

The Reich was hammered by constant attacks from the air. During the past year victories at sea had become rare events. Our once victorious army fought a seemingly endless battle while slowly retreating toward the Reich. Nazi propaganda insistence that Germany was "only shortening the front lines" made jesters whisper in gallows humor fashion that with such short front lines Hitler would need only one of his new wonder weapons to kill both the Russians and the Americans with a single stroke.

The new year started just right, at least for this student. On our first day at school the principal announced that our school was closed until further notice. He also told us that all boys were to report to city hall. There we were organized into alert teams to help unload ambulance trains that arrived almost daily from the Eastern Front. We even received military-gray German Army uniforms. Mine was a bit too large, but both Lothar and I thought it should make a good impression on the girls. Fortunately, the pair of laced army boots issued to me was better than anything I had worn in many years. Those boots alone made me feel almost like a real soldier. My sister's school, also closed, was readied to become a field hospital. Her first school year was a short one — poor girl. For reasons incomprehensible to me, she had enjoyed school enormously. Alas, her schooling lasted but three short months.

Wounded soldiers most often received their first expert medical care in a field hospital. By late 1944 the military situation had indeed become very fluid. Front line aid stations stopped the bleeding, bandaged wounds, and sedated the wounded to prevent shock. My home town had become a front line field hospital. It had also become the town's sad mission to bury those for whom help came too late. Lothar and I, along with about thirty others, were assigned to unload hospital trains arriving from the Eastern Front.

It was the 10th of January 1945, my mother's birthday, when we had our first alert. On a dark, overcast day we stood excitedly in the cold freight depot waiting for "our" train. Finally it arrived! Large clouds of white steam engulfed us. Each car had large red crosses painted on the sides and the roof. We hurried aboard. A terrible, almost unbearable, stench of ether and blood and rotting flesh hit our nostrils. Wounded were everywhere. Left and right of the aisle, in racks three high, lay pale young men with horrible wounds, with holes ripped into their bodies, with limbs shot away; many rested sedated on narrow cots covered with dark, dried bloodstains. Maggots were eating the flesh at the wound — the nurses said it prevented gangrene from further damaging the lads. They were left that way until proper care could be given in our hospital. The nurses, actually teenage girls and very young women, were fabulous. Although they were terribly exhausted, they were never too tired to wipe a brow or comfort a weary body.

Soon it became almost routine. Trains pulled in, were serviced, and departed once again for the front. They usually arrived in the early afternoon. Some, delayed by enemy action, arrived in the late evening hours — even deep into the night. When that happened we waited, apprehensively, in the freight manager's war office — sometimes in vain. On those occasions our haggard doctor stood waiting and worrying on the platform. He walked anxiously back and forth, nervously slapping his arms on his skinny body for warmth. He was always there in his captain's uniform that looked two sizes too large. When the train pulled into the station he ordered the lights in the freightyard turned on — it drove the air raid wardens wild. The boys loved him. They heard him tell the complaining chief air raid warden that to him his wounded were more valuable than all the air raid wardens in Jauer, and that if the warden would not stop bothering him he would shoot him — and the boys, and apparently the warden, believed he meant every word, because the warden never again came to the freightyard.

We had about a foot of snow on the ground. Last year we would have been sledding and skiing; no time for that now. Freightyard personnel installed potbellied stoves in the freight hall where the wounded were sorted. We fed the walking wounded, carted the ambulatory to the hospital, and placed the dead in the hall next door — the ice-cold one. The next days they would be laid to rest in our cemeteries with full military honors rendered by a squad of over-aged World War One veterans who fired the three volleys over the graves.

I remember one of those dreadful days. We had sat waiting since the early morning hours around the warm potbellied stoves. Every ten or fifteen minutes one of us rotated to the platform as lookout. Finally, we heard, "There it is!" We rushed to the edge of the platform as the engine, belching clouds of white steam, slowly rolled past. Two grim railroaders, one with a bloodstained head bandage, gave us tired waves from behind sandbags in their engine cab. The brakes shrieked loud as the train slowly came to a halt. Although each car had a large white square and a red cross painted on its side, bullet holes had shattered windows and punctured walls. Most of the windows had been hastily repaired with blankets or mattresses to stave off the bitterly cold wind. As happens so often in the confusion of war, the train had run through a station already captured by the Soviets. The crew had opened the throttle wide, shoveled in extra coals, and run through the station while surprised Red Army soldiers poured automatic rifle fire into the train.

Employees of the German State Railway were the unsung heroes of World War Two. Most were in their late forties and fifties, some even in their sixties. Most were veterans of the First World War. For some five years they had braved bombings and machine gunning by Allied planes and worked ungodly hours. Now they drove freight and passenger trains through areas near or in the combat zone. Until the very last day of the war their trains went toward the front lines with supplies and ammunition and returned with refugees and wounded soldiers.

The nurses on these ambulance trains, all in their late teens and early twenties, were wonderfully heroic. Although these young women had just ridden through heavy enemy fire, they kept up the spirits of the wounded with coarse jokes, light reprimands, and caring touches. I have one of those moments etched in my memory. We climbed aboard to unload a stretcher. A "walking wounded" with his right arm missing, shouted, "Hey sister, I am right-handed. How do I wipe my ass?"

"You are right-handed? Use your right foot," said one of the nurses. Everyone still conscious laughed.

"You think that's possible?"

"Listen," she replied, "the Führer said, 'For a German soldier, nothing is impossible.' Nothing!" Again wild laughter, soldiers' gallows humor.

I and the other three teenage litter bearers flushed with embarrassment. We carefully lifted the next stretcher and carried its precious cargo onto the platform and then into the ambulance.

Soon another ambulance train arrived. This one was unmarked and covered in camouflage paint. The flatbed car in front of the engine had a steel windbreak in front and rows of sandbags on both sides to protect the quadruple 20-millimeter antiaircraft gun mounted in the center. The gun crew of seven, maybe eight, 16- or 17-year-old boys looked grimly through frost-covered goggles. Instead of steel helmets they had towels and scarves wrapped around their heads to protect them from the bitterly cold wind. As we started to unload the wounded two old women scrambled aboard the *Flakwaggon* with quart cans of hot soup and tea to feed "their boys." Of the wounded, only the worst cases went to the local hospital. There they changed bandages and made emergency amputations — the severed legs and arms were burned in the hospital's incinerator.

At the hospital I was taking a short break in one of the passageways when a nurse, only a few years older than I, carried a bloody leg, severed just above the knee, toward the boiler room. She held the severed leg delicately in both hands. As she brushed past me I puked on the wall, on the floor, and all over my uniform. I was still recovering, with bitter bile burning in my throat, when she came back. She looked at me with incredibly sad eyes. Gently, her small, white, and terribly bloodstained hands — the hands that had only moments ago carried a part of a soldier's body — touched my tousled hair lovingly. She guided me into the laundry room. There, with a wet, refreshingly cold rag she silently wiped my face and my uniform. I wept unashamedly. Then we walked back into the brisk cold and watched as a gaunt, unshaven doctor briefly examined each arriving stretcher case. The living went to the hospital, the dead to the warehouse.

There was no letup. Ambulance train after ambulance train arrived, was serviced, and left again. The Breslau-Jauer track was one of the few not under constant air attack by American or British bombers. From here trains were routed southward through the mountain passes into Czechoslovakia and then westward to Austria and Bavaria. All the other railroad routes led directly westward toward either Dresden or Berlin-Magdeburg, areas under constant Allied bombardment.

I most enjoyed treating the walking wounded at the railroad station with hot grog, a good hot stew, and plenty of fresh, buttered bread. As soon as the train was cleaned, we loaded the wounded who had been serviced at the field hospital the previous day and they steamed southwestward into the interior of the Reich. Some of the less seriously wounded remained at the station. They asked for rides back to their fighting units to be with their comrades — they called it "deserting to the front."

The camaraderie, the togetherness of the town's people and "their wounded lads," was heartwarming. Equipped with mops, rags, brooms, and soap, ladies from the women's auxiliary of the Nazi party, and girls from the *Bund Deutscher Mädchen* stood ready to clean the compartments of blood, excrement, fleas, lice, and the dirt of muddy combat boots. Old men and women, some in their seventies, came to the station with quart cans, the enameled carriers in which they fetched their daily milk from stores. They carried hot soup or stew and black bread. At the station they eagerly fed the wounded and their helpers. A five-man band of veterans from the First World War played soft music, and small children brought little bouquets of pine branches still decorated with Christmas ornaments.

Too soon another train arrived to be serviced. This one was all shot up. The rear platform of one car was shot away; the engine had lost its smoke stack. The old-timers in the engine cab had machine guns mounted in the sandbag-protected openings that once were windows. Today's wounded had been in battle only yesterday. The front was moving closer. We relinquished our grim task only when physically and mentally exhausted.

Part Three

Götterdämmerung
(Apocalypse)

Chapter 8

The Omen

Silesians were a superstitious people. They believed in old proverbs, in ghosts and goblins, and in nature's signs — storms and dark clouds that foretold dismal events. Soothsayers predicted a terrible end for the Fatherland.

The winter of 1944–1945 was a particularly cold one. Bitter winds whipped snow from the Polish plains into Silesia. About two feet of snow covered the ground. Snow covered ditches and along hedges snow drifts four to six feet high were a common occurrence. Shortly after we celebrated the arrival of the new year one catastrophe followed another. Then we heard what was, for Silesians, the most horrifying news.

> Achtung, achtung, Das Oberkommando
> der Wehrmacht gibt bekannt.
>
> 13 January 1945. The long-expected Soviet winter offensive on the Vistula Front[1] has commenced. The enemy attacked with numerous rifle and tank divisions from the Baranow bridgehead after an extraordinarily heavy artillery barrage. Bitter fighting has ensued. Companion attacks south and north of this sector were repulsed.[2]

I wonder now whether we recalled Preuss Oma's predictions that terrible events would befall us. She had read the future from the twisted lead that formed during last New Year's Eve's lead poring. In fact, on the 12th of January 1945 the Soviets had launched a devastating, all-out attack along the entire Eastern Front from the Baltic Sea in the north to the Carpathian Mountains in the south. The Soviets virtually obliterated the German line in eastern Poland. By 17 January 1945 the situation in the Vistula area had become critical. The enemy had inserted some 90 rifle divisions and 15 tank corps into the battle. During bitter combat the enemy armor points penetrated all the way to the area northeast of Krakow. These armor columns had bypassed slow-moving German units that continued to fight their way in "walking encirclements" until reunited with their units or until they were totally annihilated.[3] After Soviet armor had bypassed many of the larger cities the German High Command declared cities such as Posen, Graudenz, and Breslau "fortresses." These fortresses fought until either out of ammunition or completely overwhelmed by superior enemy forces.

Once Soviet armor had pierced the German Main Line of Resistance (MLR) the enemy did not stop to mop up German Army remnants. In fact, the Soviets' advance did not stop until it was forced to regroup at the Oder River. They had used German *Blitzkrieg* tactics rather successfully. It was lack of fuel and ammunition not German resistance that caused this halt.

As a consequence of this massive Soviet attack we first noticed a trickle of refugees from the east. These refugees—the well-to-do—came by automobile, by train, and in horse-drawn wagons. It all appeared very orderly. They remained at most a day or two to rest then wandered farther westward. Later the first passenger trains loaded with frightened refugees careened through our railroad station. Terrified little faces stared through frost-covered windows. These trains stopped only if coal or water had to be replenished. They were routed westward toward Dresden and beyond.

While others fled we still had to service the wounded on the ambulance trains. It was not only physically exhausting, it also strained everyone mentally. I did not know how much longer I could stand the blood and grime. Once, totally exhausted, I sought solace in the horse stable where the damp warmth, the familiar smells of ammonia and horses and hay and oats restored my sanity. I called to Stutti, the slender dark-brown mare with black mane and long tail. She, and the others, turned their heads. I walked up to the trough, gently scratched her throat and lower lip and said, "Stutti, be glad you are not a human." She nodded her head as if she understood the essence of my thought. The others were waiting. I called each one by name, walked up, and caressed them. I knew horses. They had kept me dry when, as a little boy, I hid from rain squalls under their bellies; they had warmed my legs during long rides through wintry fields; and they had listened many times to my outpouring of problems with girls or school. They understood. Especially now, I could not talk to Mother, nor with any other adult, about the horrors of the hospital train, about the wounded, the dying, and the dead. Only my friends, the horses, were understanding listeners.

> Achtung, achtung, Das Oberkommando
> der Wehrmacht gibt bekannt.
>
> 18 January 1945. The battle in the large bend of the Vistula River continues with unabated force. Reserves brought to the front have slowed enemy attacks between Krakow and Tschenstochau.[4]

When we heard that Soviet armor had reached Krakow, the announcement sent shock waves through our community. Krakow was not all that far away. Although everything else had the appearance of normality, those few locals who mistrusted the Nazi government started discreet preparations for departure. They mailed large packages of precious possessions to relatives or friends in the western part of the Reich, then departed quietly. Some had saved enough fuel to drive their automobiles, others simply boarded a scheduled train never to return. Our two Protestant ministers and their families were among the wise departees. Alas, the three Catholic priests remained with their flock. They were beaten, and two were rumored killed, defending women of their flock against Soviet rapists.

After the collapse of the Eastern Front the horrors of war descended on Jauer. Disaster had struck East Prussia in late 1944, now it was our turn. On 24 January 1945 our alert teams received additional duties. We were divided into traffic control and antiaircraft crews. Lothar and I became traffic guides. We directed the steadily increasing refugee traffic. Others manned antiaircraft guns atop buildings. We received carbines and a basic load of ammunition. In addition to directing traffic, we now guarded the outskirts of town against marauding gangs of foreign forced laborers; we were in fact the local police force. The last of the able police officers, i.e., the one who walked without a cane, had departed for the front north and east of town. The town garrison was empty. A sergeant, my former riding instructor, returned from Steinau-on-Oder, where Jauer's noncommissioned officers' school was to make its last stand, to get ammunition from the depot. He left with three horse-drawn sleds loaded to capacity with small arms ammunition. Not the German Army, but deteriorating logistics, stopped the Russian steamroller at the Oder

PART THREE—*Götterdämmerung* (Apocalypse)

River. After a short rest they regrouped and plunged westward with renewed vigor. Now all hope for the Fatherland was lost!

In early February the eastern sky was lit from flashes of big guns. Each night the rolling thunder of war came closer. Ever more trainloads of wounded arrived for transshipment. I had already lost all illusions of glamour and heroics depicted so cleverly in magazines and newsreels. There was nothing beautiful, nor was there anything good about war, only gut-tearing sorrow seeing young men and women each in his or her private hell. Nazi propaganda had frequently mentioned that German forces were pulling back "to shorten the front lines." By early 1945 even the most loyal of Nazis recognized that the end of the "Thousand-Year Reich" was near. Yet, the Nazi government did not evacuate the civilian population in time to prevent disaster. Frantic, desperate refugees arrived from east of the Oder River. Then came terrified refugees from west of the Oder River through Jauer. Eventually that flow of refugees became a flood. Among the refugees were British and French prisoners of war released from their POW camps. We housed them all, provided food and drink and a warm place to sleep, fed their horses, and then sent them on their way into an uncertain future. Trains careened through the station. They stopped only to replenish coal or water. *Treks* (wagon trains) filled all streets leading southward toward the mountains into Czechoslovakia. The weather had worsened. Drifting snow with ice-crusted edges covered ditches, fence rows, and hedges. Only the darkness of the wartime blackout and the need to feed and rest the horses forced these terrified people to seek shelter. We guided them to local farms and fed people and horses. Women, children, and a few old men slept together with their horses and oxen in our barns. They hurriedly left as the first light of dawn appeared on the horizon. We looked at their sad lot — creaky wagons loaded with small children and old women — and knew that soon we would join them in flight.

The Soviets were using the *Blitzkrieg* tactics that the Germans had used so successfully only three or four years earlier. The German Army, fighting a bitter, desperate battle to protect the Fatherland, was totally outnumbered. Some 3.1 million Germans with 28,500 guns and mortars, 4,000 tanks and self-propelled guns (tank killers), and about 1,960 combat aircraft, faced 11.5 million Russians with 108,000 guns and mortars, 12,900 tanks and self-propelled guns, and 15,540 aircraft.

Opposite: **Silesian peasant fleeing from the Soviets, 24 February 1945.** *Author's diary.*

Chapter 9

Distant Thunder

> Kill, Kill! The Germans are innocent of nothing; not those alive, and not those yet to be born. Follow the orders of Comrade Stalin and smash forever the German beast in his burrow. Break with force the racial arrogance of the German women. Take them as your rightful plunder. Kill, you bravely advancing Red Army soldiers.[1]
> — Soviet Poet Ilja Ehrenburg, exhorting the soldiers

The Eastern Front once again gained prominence in the official announcements from the German High Command. Searching the map for the many place names mentioned one could determine the seriousness of this attack. German units encircled by the enemy in Poland, East Prussia, and Silesia — some maybe a hundred miles behind the enemy line — fought tenaciously until reunited with the core of the army or until totally destroyed.

> Achtung, achtung. Das Oberkommando der Wehrmacht gibt bekannt.
> 1 February 1945. Addendum: Lance Corporal Schurz of the noncommissioned officers' school in Jauer has on 27 January within three hours destroyed four tanks with his Panzerfaust.[2]

Another proud accomplishment by our home town unit trying to hold back the Red Menace. But all these heroics had little impact on the military situation. During the last week of January weak German forces held the front between Maltsch and Liegnitz against Soviet forces attacking from the north-northeast. *Volkssturm*[3] Battalion Jauer deployed there and suffered its first casualties. The enemy made quick advances as a second wave of overwhelming Soviet forces launched a large-scale attack. This attack broke through the line and the Soviets gained ground rapidly.[4] Little of this was known to the citizens of Jauer. Apparently, the local Nazis knew that the Führer did not look kindly on "defeatists" and feared to be targeted as such. Grandfather believed neither what the local Nazis nor the national leadership had to say about the status of the war, but even he found it difficult to accept that the situation had deteriorated to such an extent that it would cause him to lose his farm, his fields, his animals, his entire way of life. When Grandfather heard that the Soviets had forced the crossing of the Oder River at Steinau he decided that, no matter what the local Nazis decreed, it was prudent to prepare for flight. Four of the large horse-drawn wagons that had just a few months ago hauled sugar beets were cleaned, their axles were carefully lubricated, and canvas covers were spread over wooden spars to protect the passengers and their cargo from the elements. The six horses and the two oxen received additional feed to strengthen them for the anticipated hardship of pulling heavily laden wagons through steep mountain passes. Harnesses were carefully inspected for flaws; they were carefully rubbed with leather-softening oils. The blacksmith fitted all the horses with horseshoes that had screw-in H-shaped spikes for superb traction on icy roads. The wagons were loaded with the best linen, clothing, food, and feed. Everything was ready. Only the timing for the departure had to be carefully calculated. The local Nazis still controlled the roads. The appearance of deserting the town or having a defeatist attitude had to be avoided at all cost.

My Onkel[5] Arthur, a farmer and part-time mayor of Lobris, a small village a few miles to the east, had his family join the clan. Tante Kläre and her children, along with André, a French prisoner of war who drove the wagon, joined us in Jauer. Onkel Arthur could not be with them; the county government had appointed him *Kampfkommandant*[6] Lobris, the man in charge of defending the village, in Arthur's opinion an utterly ridiculous and meaningless title. Under his "command" a few old farmers were to stop the Soviet steamroller at the gates of their little village. Everyone was threatened under penalty of death "to stand and fight." Grandfather thought this to be another one of the inventions of the Greatest Field Marshal of All Times. Neither Onkel Arthur nor his fellow farmers had any intention, or the capability, to mount any type of defense.

Sometime in the first week of February 1945 we started to hear the steady thunder of guns. All through the night we saw flashes all along the eastern and northern sky. Large and small army units and splinter groups arrived. If there could be total chaos, it was here. Although our roads were clogged with slow-moving civilian horse- or oxen-drawn covered wagons, handcarts, bicycles, we had not yet received orders, i.e., permission, to evacuate.

> Achtung, achtung, Das Oberkommando der Wehrmacht gibt bekannt.
> 6 February 1945. Addendum: The noncommissioned officers' school, Jauer, Colonel Reichard commanding, has heroically defended the town of Steinau for five days against attacks by overwhelming enemy infantry and armor units. Only when all ammunition was depleted has this brave crew fought its way back to our own lines as ordered.[7]

On the 10th of February 1945 we heard from a nun, who had survived rape and the murder of her sisters, that our Unteroffizierschule Jauer at the Steinau-on-Oder bridgehead had met with disaster, that the defenders had been decimated. At the police station she told us proudly that "when the boys from Jauer died in the ruins of Steinau, there was not one stone left atop another." We also learned that only a small group from the NCO academy had managed to escape; almost everyone else was killed defending that important Oder River crossing.

This Soviet breakthrough opened the sluice gates for strong enemy forces to advance into Lower Silesia. Retribution for past sins descended on all Germans: on those who had wholeheartedly supported the regime, on those who had lived in quiet desperation, and on those who had actively opposed the Nazis. Reports reached the OKW[8] that Soviet troops, ordered by Stalin and encouraged by such distinguished persons as the noted Soviet poet Ilja Ehrenburg "to kill, kill, and to spare no one," had followed those orders only too well. Unlike the well-organized and totally disciplined Nazis, who had systematically targeted specific categories of people for extermination, Soviet troops raped, plundered, burned, and killed civilians and soldiers indiscriminantly. Old farmers, women, and children were murdered in the most horrible ways. Grandfathers who attempted to protect their female kin were shot. Young girls, middle-aged women, and women in their eighties were repeatedly raped next to their dead men folk — and then they too were shot. Counterattacking

German infantry found them stripped of their shoes and valuables in houses, in barns and in snow-covered streets. The Soviets, in their killing frenzy, did not even spare Allied prisoners of war. French POWs working on German farms were found shot along with their German employers. Sheer terror drove the refugees from one sanctuary to another. Death came in many forms: from hunger, bitter cold, strafing fighter bombers, and Soviet tanks roaming behind German lines. Always there was the terror of being brutalized and murdered by an enemy who had been given carte blanche by his High Command.

> Achtung, achtung. Das Oberkommando
> der Wehrmacht gibt bekannt.
> 10 February 1945. The Soviets have inserted heavy combat elements in battle sector Breslau-Liegnitz-Glogau and broke through our tenacious defense and gained further territory.[9]

At that time we did not know that the Soviets had already captured Liegnitz, our district town only some 15 miles to the northwest. Neither did we know that two prongs of Soviet armor were in the process of encircling us from the east and the west. Nor did we know that most Nazis had abandoned their charges and left for safety westward.

With flight imminent, Tante Kläre begged me to take one of her horses and Grandfather's light open carriage to make a last attempt to persuade her husband to come to Jauer. My cousin Gisela came along. The 7-kilometer drive to Lobris was frightening. Whereas the road should have been crowded with people fleeing from points north and east, we were alone. Lobris was in turmoil. Old men and women stood on the village road uncertain what to do. The men were forbidden to leave and their women folk did not want to depart without them, although they had heard the horror stories of Russian atrocities. Only the Baron von Wolkenstein had disregarded orders; he and his flock had left the village several days before. He was one of those who had saved diesel fuel and used his farm tractors to pull the wagons. Tante Kläre was the only other person who had left Lobris. My trip to Lobris, my attempt to convince Onkel Arthur to leave, was unsuccessful. At parting he gave me a large pistol and some ammunition for protection. He told me, "Take care of the girls." We knew we had met for the last time. On our return trip a fighter aircraft buzzed us. I could not tell whether it was German or Soviet, because I had trouble controlling the terrified horse.

When we finally learned that Soviet forces had captured Liegnitz our clan was ready to leave on the long journey into the unknown. There was so much uncertainty. What should be taken and what must be left? All the livestock, except horses and oxen were abandoned. The dairy cows, long nurtured in stables, were incapable of traveling on hard, icy roads. All of Grandfather's pigs, geese, ducks, pigeons, and goats were abandoned. We had spent a restless night interrupted by dull explosions of artillery that foretold the approach of the front line.

Chapter 10

Flight

During early February a sudden, unusual thaw melted some of the snow that usually covered the lowlands and the foothills of the Sudeten Mountains. The fields and the tall pine trees just south of town still stood glittering in frosted glory, but city streets and country roads had turned into a dirty gray-white mess. During the night this slush froze into sharp, hard forms that made travel for bicycles, cars, tractors, and trucks, but especially for the draft horses and oxen, extremely hazardous.

> Achtung, achtung. Das Oberkommando
> der Wehrmacht gibt bekannt.
>
> 12 February 1945. The battle in Lower Silesia increases in dimensions.... From their bridgehead at Brieg enemy forces are streaming northwestward.... North of Bunzlau, east of Sagan there is heavy fighting.... In the past four weeks of the winter offensive units of the Army, the Waffen SS, and the Luftwaffe's antiaircraft and flying elements have destroyed 7,966 tanks, many hundreds of guns, in excess of 10,000 motorized and horse-drawn vehicles. Also destroyed either in the air or on the ground were 457 aircraft.[1]

The official broadcasts did not mention that on 11 February Soviet forces advanced from Goldberg and reached the northern edge of the County Jauer line.[2] That evening my classmate Lothar Scholz[3] and I, along with the rest of the police and Hitler Youth defense teams, met at city hall to await further orders and news from the front. In an inspiring speech Jauer's mayor and ardent Nazi party member, acting as the *Kampfkommandant*, told how the Army, the *Volkssturm*, and all other able bodied men and boys would defend Jauer "shoulder-to-shoulder to our last breath." He ordered us to assemble at city hall at noon the following day so that he could lead us into battle to save our homes from the dreaded "Red Beasts."

For eons my ancestors had fought and died defending this little place on earth we called home. Now there was no one left but lame old men and fourteen-, fifteen- and sixteen-year-old boys. It was part bravado, adventurousness, foolishness, but also obligation, love for the soil, and the unrealistic hope that if we really tried hard, things would turn out all right. There also was the foolish and totally unrealistic belief that somehow the Soviets would stop just short of our beloved town. Totally nonsensical, but ...

Before dawn broke on the 12th of February 1945 the Thamm family hastily harnessed horses and oxen to covered wagons. Stutti sensed the emergency. Her long black tail whipped back and forth. As I harnessed her she pawed the ground with her left front hoof. With the unfamiliar cracks of artillery shells exploding in the distance she laid her ears back, then raised them upward. Under the light of kerosene lanterns casting eerie shadows over the glistening ice-covered cobblestones I led her into the dark farmyard. The Thamms, the Lachmanns, the Baumerts, and the Scholzes mounted the covered wagons. Grandfather raised up from the lead wagon, glanced around for a last time at the property he had nurtured for half a century, and cracked his whip. Startled, the first team of horses bolted before leaning into their harnesses. Stutti turned her head toward me. I raced to her side to give her one last pat. Standing alone in the farmyard Lothar and I waved as the wagon train departed through the large wrought-iron gate into the street.

Just before our *Trek* departed, my mother begged me to leave with them. The Ukrainian women farm laborers pleaded; they were sure the Russians would kill me, but I simply could not run away, could not abandon my home town without a fight — or so I thought.

From the north we heard the unrelenting rumble of artillery fire. Unfamiliar with judging the combat scene, the closeness of detonations and flashes of exploding ordnance, Lothar and I reported to the *Rathaus*[3] as ordered. Before climbing the stairs to the guard room we walked into the *Rathskeller*[4]. There was no one there, not a living soul, empty. Food lay on the counter — bread and sausages, bottle upon bottle of beer readily available under the bar. We gathered up enough to feed ten. As we walked into the police station we saw the old police officer, the only one left in town, staring out of the open window overlooking the road where just yesterday an unending stream of refugee wagons had rushed past city hall. He looked a hundred years old. He had been at the station for the past week, sleeping whenever he could on an army cot in the otherwise empty holding cell. He had lived on cigarettes and coffee and the occasional plate of food we boys fetched from the restaurant below. The room reeked of cigarette smoke, wet wool, shoe polish, old leather, and unwashed bodies. He ate the food we brought hungrily, yet unenthusiastically. We had known him now for almost a month and thought him to be a widower, although he had never spoken of his family. The telephone rang incessantly; he waved his hand and between bites he told us not to answer it. There was nothing we could do anymore for anybody. Lothar asked the old man whether he had heard anything from the front. Any news? The police officer told him to stick his head out the window and Lothar would hear all the news he wanted to hear. "The Russians will be here shortly," he said, "and you boys had better get going or those bastards will cut your throats."

He heaved himself erect, wiped his mouth with the back of the sleeve of his tunic, hobbled over to the coat rack, and laboriously climbed into his slate-colored greatcoat. He carefully buttoned it, snapped his pistol belt and shoulder harness together, retrieved four full magazines for his pistol from the desk drawer, shoved one into his P-38 automatic, pulled back the operating slide, snapped a round into the chamber, and, with a swift motion based on many years of weapons handling, flipped the safety lever to safe. The other magazines went into his left overcoat pocket. In his parting remarks he told us of two motorcycles in the staircase below the guardroom. He would take one, the other one was for us. He cautioned us not to let anyone stop us. The Nazi scum, the brownshirts, had already flown the coop. Our startled looks made him pause momentarily, contemplating what he had just said. Then he looked up and added that the bastards had talked big, even the previous night, but that this very morning, he contemptuously spit out the word *Kampfkommandant*— that this morning the Herr *Kampfkommandant* and his minions had gotten into their big cars and left us holding the bag.

He paused again, sighted, pointed at the weapons locker, and told us to take the machine pistols and plenty of ammo and if one of those bastard brownshirts should try to stop us, to kill him! With words akin to "Take the guns and the ammo, and, the good Lord willing, I'll see you up in the mountains. Better yet, in Bavaria where the Ami[5] will soon be.

Good luck," he limped into the hallway. Still in shock at hearing a German police officer speaking ill of Nazi party members, we listened to his heavy footsteps going down the marble stairs, and shortly thereafter the light clatter of a motorcycle.

We looked at each other. We were alone. From the sound it appeared that artillery explosions were coming nearer. The telephone rang again. We ignored it. Then Lothar walked over to the gun locker, lifted out a machine pistol, grabbed a cluster of nine belted magazines, rammed an extra one into the gun, and said, "Let's go!" I reached over and took the other machine pistol from the rack, also slung a heavy belt with nine magazines over my skinny shoulders, and loaded the extra magazine. I had never realized how heavy this armament could be. As we walked out of the building, almost as an afterthought, Lothar said over his shoulder, "Let's get something good to eat at the farm before we head into the mountains and Bolkenhain."

Lothar started the motorcycle and I climbed on the seat behind him. I never knew that Lothar could handle a motorcycle. We rode leisurely through empty streets to the farm as if there were not a single worry in the whole wide world. The huge iron gates of the farm, usually securely locked, stood ajar. Cows, goats, sheep, and pigs were left behind in their stables. Chickens, ducks, and geese eagerly explored the farmyard for leftover food. It was calm, except for the rumble of artillery fire coming from the north. It was high noon.

Unbeknown to us, sixteen Soviet T-34 medium tanks, accompanied by infantry rolled toward my home town. They had already broken through elements of General Wagner's 269th Infantry (Hamburg) Division and swept away remnants of the 100th Jäger (Light Infantry) Division and Jauer's finest, the soon to be decimated *Volkssturm* Battalion. With little effort these tanks quickly dispersed the defenders from their hastily dug defensive positions along the *Chaussee*[6] just north of Grandfather's farm. The defenders skirted the town and fled southward toward the foothills of the Sudeten Mountains. A lone antiaircraft gun, an 8.8-cm Flak, in position north of the railroad station, fired only a few rounds, destroying one T-34 tank before it itself was destroyed. The surviving Flak crew retreated, now fighting as riflemen.

Meanwhile Lothar and I, feeling pretty grown-up and totally unaware of our precarious position, were in the upstairs kitchen frying bacon and eggs for lunch. Soon the bacon sputtered in the large, cast-iron pan on the gas stove — electricity, city water, and city gas still functioned normally. Lothar had just sliced some bread when tank gun or machine gun fire ripped into the roof of the residence. Broken slate roof tiles cascaded past the window and smashed to the ground below. Terrified, afraid to use the doors, thinking that Soviet infantry had already entered the farm, we hastily exited the kitchen through the second floor window onto the roof of the porch and jumped from there to the ground. It was not quite as bad as we thought, but Soviet tanks were indeed less than 500 yards from the farm on the Liegnitzer Chaussee. This was not the heroic "baptism of fire" we had so often admired in the cinema. Frantically Lothar attempted to start the motorcycle he had so judiciously parked in the driveway. He stepped repeatedly on the kick starter. Nothing. The engine coughed but did not start. In his panic he had forgotten to turn the ignition switch. Finally, with the switch turned properly, the motor coughed, then stuttered, and finally roared into life. We sped out of the farm. Above us was the wild firing of machine guns and cannons — German and Soviet fighter planes engaged in battle. Trying to hide under the bare branches of the chestnut trees, and disregarding all traffic rules, we rode on the sidewalk along the cemetery wall, then between the cemetery wall and a large barn. Just as we emerged into the open road leading from the railroad station southward to the *Neumarkt*[7] a horrendous explosion tore apart the tall railroad switching tower. We thought the Russians were already in the next city block. Unbeknown to us, and at the very last moment before the Soviets arrived, German engineers had immobilized the shunting yard. We thought all was lost. Now, only flight could save us. We raced southward past the market square. The roar of our motorcycle startled people impatiently standing or sitting on suitcases waiting for transportation. We shouted, "The Russians are right behind us! Run!" Some in that group looked up angrily as if they had just heard a bad joke, others stared in disbelief. After all, had not the Nazi party promised to evacuate them? Frantically, we continued our flight; now it was everyone for himself!

We crossed the Wütende Neisse, the mountain stream where we had so joyfully played and washed our horses only a few months ago, and rode southward toward the next village. There seemed to be some confusion ahead. At the southern edge of town large ambulances — converted buses — partially blocked the road. Nurses, doctors, and soldiers rushed in and out of the auxiliary hospital carrying wounded on stretchers into the ambulances. Standing in the road and blocking all traffic stood a tall, slender, unshaven doctor — our hero from the ambulance train days — still in his two-sizes-too-large uniform and waving a large pistol. He stopped all those in uniform and forced them to load his wounded lads. We stopped, Lothar leaned his motorcycle against a stone wall, and we ran into the hospital to lend a hand. A short time later one of the young nurses shouted from the second floor that the last of the wounded was on the ground floor. The doctor raced into the building for a final check. He emerged quickly with a grateful smile spreading across his stubbled face. He shouted a loud, "Thank you, thank you, everyone." He swung himself aboard as the last of the ambulances finally cleared the gate; all that remained was a cloud of heavy diesel exhaust smoke.

Heavily armed men once again walked southward. We, on our motorcycle, rode along the fruit tree–bordered country lane. Above the engine noise of our motorcycle we heard a strange, wobbling sound soon followed by several distant explosions. It was the sound of artillery shells fired from worn-out Soviet tubes, the first I had ever heard — or seen; one could actually see the projectiles as they passed overhead. The shells exploded some distance across our road of escape. Undeterred the ambulances and buses rolled through the artillery impact area. We followed somewhat reluctantly. With a loud clap of thunder fountains of dirt and snow rose into the air repeatedly. Momentarily they looked like rows of black poplar trees; then they collapsed into dirty, smoking scars in the snow. Again and again explosions tore into the road and the adjacent fields, yet, no one stopped to take cover — escape was of the essence. To our rear a dozen Soviet tanks and infantry, in front a blistering artillery barrage, and above us German and Soviet fighter aircraft battling for dominance. The thunder of aircraft engines from German Messerschmitt fighters and Soviet JABOs.[8] The dry stutter of their cannons and machine guns, the screech of high velocity shells, and their slower companions from the artillery, the hard report of explosions in leafless trees and on the road, and the staccato of antiaircraft fire that German infantry poured into the sky. Standing orders were: everyone fires on incoming enemy aircraft — with pistols, rifles, and machine guns. This was the cacophony of war, a totally unforgettable experience.

There were wide-open meadows to the left and the right of the road. Every time we heard the howl of aircraft engines most of us jumped into the wet and filthy drainage ditches on both sides of the country road. There we waited until the aircraft was directly overhead, so low you could almost touch it. Then I raised my machine pistol and fired the entire magazine straight into the air without looking or bothering to aim. The crescendo disoriented some. Cowering in the drainage ditch, hip-deep in dirty snow and water, out of the corner of my eye I saw a soldier standing in the middle of the road shaking his fist and cursing the aircraft. Others fired their weapons without bothering to take cover. I saw another soldier firing his pistol, squeezing the trigger long after the last round had left the barrel and the operating slide had jammed in the open position.

I jerked the empty magazine out of my gun. With frozen, fumbling fingers I tore at the leather cover of the reserve magazine harness. I pressed the full magazine into the gun, pulled back the operating slide just as another aircraft made its attack run. Terrified I ducked down into the slushy snow, raised the machine pistol, and squeezed the trigger just as the shadow of an aircraft passed overhead. Another thirty-plus rounds of 9-mm parabellum projectiles shattered the air. Time and again the JABOs flew along the road and let loose unending bursts of steel; they fired on anything that moved — or did not. Time and again I loaded a magazine and emptied its contents into the sky. With thousands of rounds fired at us, I saw not one person wounded or killed. During a lull I looked around. Lothar lay in the snow face down. He did not move. *Oh God*, I thought, *he is dead*. I hesitantly tugged on his sleeve, gently, then harder. He moved. He raised his head, somewhat embarrassed. His machine pistol was half-buried in the snow. It had not been fired at all. He tried to make light of it, but it did not matter. We were both totally scared out of our wits. Maybe some good came from his reluctance to fire recklessly into the sky: I was almost out of ammunition, his magazine harness was still full. We had lost count of the number of times the ground attack aircraft had forced us to jump into the dirty drainage ditches. Twenty-millimeter aircraft shells exploded in the branches of the apple trees and their hot, empty cartridges fell on the road. Almost directly overhead a fighter plane disintegrated in a terrifying explosion. Pieces of metal and flesh fell in a wide swath. From the west a twin-engine Messerschmitt 110 long-range fighter came in low, trailing smoke. The rear gunner jumped. Too late! His parachute flared. He slammed into a bridge railing. Twitching pieces of bone and flesh lay in the dirty road. The ME-110 made a smooth landing in the meadow about a mile away, but the pilot remained in the aircraft; he too was dead. The last time we climbed out of the drainage ditch Lothar attempted to start the motorcycle. No luck. Disgusted he gave it a shove and it slid into the ditch. Now we walked like all the others.

During a sudden, almost unreal, lull in the firing we rushed through the shell-cratered area. To our left was the town's dairy. Artillery fire or not, we stopped to stuff a pound or more of butter into our knapsacks — soldiers never know where the next meal will come from. In the distance I could just barely make out the first buildings of the next village. Before us stretched a long line of hastily retreating soldiers, unorganized, disorderly, without leadership. Lothar and I found it difficult to keep up with the others. To our rear was an almost empty road on which we imagined the Soviets were rapidly advancing. Suddenly, from far back we heard the roar of diesels. We hurried, we tried to run — it could only be Soviet tanks. The noise grew into a steady roar as three army trucks emerged from the edge of the town we had just left. German Army trucks! We waved. The first truck stopped. Lothar and I tried to climb aboard; only he made it. I lost my footing. First my gun, then I fell onto the road. The truck careened away. The second truck swerved around me, but, mercifully, the third stopped. The driver shouted, "Get in back." This time I recklessly threw my gun into the cargo space first and followed quickly. With a roar the truck picked up speed. I had just caught my breath when a fighter plane thundered across our vehicle. It was so low that the rush of air lifted and tore on the tarpaulin; the entire truck rocked back and forth like a ship in heavy seas. For a long moment I stayed crouched in the narrow space between large gray boxes and the tailgate too scared, or too tired, to move. When I finally gathered my senses I saw the stenciled writing on the crates: *Faustpatrone* — antitank rocket — better known as *Panzerfaust*[9] — the rifleman's hallelujah weapon.[10] There is an old German Army proverb that proclaims that "a bad ride is better than a good walk." It had undoubtedly been coined by someone who had never ridden through a hail of bullets on a truck loaded with highly volatile rockets.

Through small villages the truck labored southward, steadily climbing through the tree-covered foothills of the Sudeten Mountains. Totally exhausted, despite the cold and the rumbling of the diesel, I had fallen asleep. Startled, I was awakened by shouts, the grinding of gears, and the squealing of brakes. The truck came to a shuddering halt. Someone ripped open the truck's tailgate. From the mouth of the meanest-looking, dirt-covered face under a camouflage-white steel helmet came the command, "Get out, get out, fast!"

I thought *Thank the Lord, it's German*, as I scrambled from the truck.

Chapter 10— Flight

Along the road some distance away stood a tough-looking lieutenant and three other men in mud-smeared uniforms, their machine-pistols at the ready pointing at the trucks and at a group of German soldiers. *Feldpolizei*— military police, also known as "Chaindogs."[11]

The Chaindogs were the toughest of the tough. Their officers had summary execution authority: any deserter could be shot without trial, with just a scant notice in the officer's daily log book. Sometimes they carried the Führer's edict that "There is no one too good to die for Germany," a bit too far, but, on the other hand, these were desperate times and the Chaindogs got the job done. They assembled all able-bodied men, formed them into combat teams, and returned them to the fighting front. It was here that the remnants of the 269th Infantry Division were to make their stand, or die, stopping the Soviet onslaught — and the Chaindogs were here to make sure every soldier did his duty. The lieutenant looked at me only slightly amused. "How old are you?" he asked.

"Fif ... fif ... fifteen! ... Sir!" I stuttered.

The lieutenant grabbed me by the bottom of my trousers and the top of my collar and with one swift motion he threw me back on the truck. One of the soldiers whipped my machine pistol from the truck bed and slammed shut the tailgate. With a wave of his machine pistol the diesel roared back to life and the truck continued its southward journey. I sat shivering in the corner between the rocket crates and the back gate and watched as a small group of tired soldiers marched northward toward the front. And I was ashamed, because I was so terribly glad not to be marching with them.

Chapter 11

Retreat into the Sudeten Mountains

Dusk settled quickly over the Sudeten Mountains. The truck continued its climb through narrow serpentine mountain roads. Totally exhausted from running, but mostly from being afraid, I had again fallen asleep; the roar of the diesel and the motion of the truck were my lullaby. It was dark as we arrived at Bolkenhain, a little town that had guarded the strategic mountain pass from Bohemia into the Silesian lowlands for almost a millennium. An old fortress, curving mountain roads, and high cliffs had protected this town from marauders for nearly a thousand years. During springs of the past few years I had camped here with the German Boy Scouts on a hill overlooking the town and the fortress.

The local quartermaster awaited the battered troops with food, dry blankets, and quarters in a warm movie theater. There was a cover of straw spread between the seats; hot drinks and bread were served by the women's auxiliary of the Nazi party and girls from the *Bund Deutscher Mädchen*. I met Lothar at the door of the theater; he had arrived just minutes earlier. Only now did we realize how soaking wet and incredibly dirty we were. The quartermaster gave us dry socks and long, scratchy, woolen army underwear. We hung our uniforms, footrags,[1] and boots to dry on the theater's hot radiators and sat, wrapped in blankets, sipping hot chocolate. Later, still in long underwear and wrapped in gray army blankets, we went into the theater lobby for a bowl of the greatest potato soup we had ever eaten. Then we slept.

The Chaindogs had apparently gathered enough combatants to stop the advancing Soviets, who had captured Goldberg and Jauer. Here, along the Katzbach Mountains (the foothills of the Sudeten Mountains) and the Wütende Neisse River, the Soviets met bitter resistance; their attack was stopped.[2] The situation, however, was still critical because *Heeresgruppe Mitte* (Army Group Center) had lost all of its reserves. To make matters worse, General von Xylander, its commander, had been shot down over Dresden on his way to report the seriousness of the situation to Hitler. He had planned to tell the Führer that the *Heeresgruppe* was unable to defend the Oder River line, unable to break through and relieve the encircled fortresses of Breslau and Glogau, and that its left flank, covered by the 17th Army, had large undefended gaps between Striegau and Jauer. The good news was that *Heeresgruppe* counterattacks managed to halt the Soviets along the line Striegau-Schweidnitz-Jauer.[3]

The lights in the theater never dimmed. New arrivals, careful not to awaken the exhausted, bedded down. I dreamt I was running through mud that had the consistency of heavy syrup. I simply could not run fast enough to get away from whatever was chasing me. The smell of strong coffee and the ambient noises of the morning awakened me. I was still terribly dirty in the morning, though I had managed to scrape off most of the mud from my uniform, which had dried during the night. Only now did I fully realize that I had escaped mortal danger, that I had escaped, that I was alive! I was alive, but not yet safe. From those who had arisen before me I learned that yesterday's Soviet armor had cut off our route of escape. Little did we know that for some time Soviet armored forces had surrounded us. We were now with remnants of the 100th Jäger Division that had broken through, and destroyed one of the Soviet pincers.

Two orders from the OKW demonstrated that Berlin did not seem to understand the seriousness of the situation here in Silesia. It issued the directive to the almost decimated Seventeenth Army to place itself in an advantageous position to launch an attack against Breslau, to reestablish contact with Fortress Breslau, and — through attack and defense — to prevent enemy breakthroughs north of Schweidnitz and enemy advances along the foothills west of Striegau, i.e., line Jauer-Goldberg.[4] The other order, dated 21 February 1945, directed *Heeresgruppe Mitte* to prevent further enemy advances past the line Görlitz-Schwedt, to keep the Silesian industrial area firmly in German hands, and to prepare for counterattacks northward along both sides of Liegnitz against the enemy's left flank. Plans were to be submitted to the High Command by 24 February 1945.[5]

To this nonsense General von Natzmer, chief of staff, and acting commander, *Heeresgruppe Mitte*, replied that he harbored no thoughts of counterattacking, that he was barely capable of maintaining his present defensive position. Furthermore, he had no reserves, and what forces became available were needed to plug existing gaps in his flanks.[6]

The main thrust of the Soviet attack was in a straight east-west direction. Initially the Soviets ignored their right flank, their southern exposure. This right flank stretched from the Upper Silesian coal fields for some hundred miles into Thuringia.

> Achtung, achtung. Das Oberkommando
> der Wehrmacht gibt bekannt.
> 23 February 1945. Along the Silesian Front between Zobten [Mountain] and Lauban the enemy pushes southward.[7]

During February and March of 1945 Soviet Army elements of the Ukrainian Front turned southward toward the Sudeten Mountains. For a short time Soviet tanks attempted to penetrate our lines, but the mountain roads, with their numerous hairpin turns and narrow passes, made armored operations extremely dangerous. Eventually the Soviets stopped all attempts to capture the region of the Sudeten Mountains; apparently they were satisfied holding a stabilized line along the foothills of these mountains.

To relieve the congestion at the entrance of this mountain pass Lothar and I, along with three or four others, received orders to keep moving into the mountains toward Landeshut, a city on the mountain pass leading into Czechoslovakia. There a hastily organized element of the VIII Korps would take care of us. It was a beautiful day for hiking. The sun was brilliant. Not a cloud was in the pale blue sky. It was cold here in the foothills, but comfortable as long as one kept moving. A heavy blanket of the most pristine snow covered the fields to the left and right of the road. Here and there we saw deer tracks. The hard snow on the road gave firm footing to the marchers. Around four in the afternoon chilly whiffs of air foretold the crispness of the coming night. An old peasant woman waved us into her house. She had a warm kitchen and a floor covered with straw. She was a most wonderful person and happy to have some soldiers in her house. We ate her soup and bread, and slept until late the next morning.

Chapter 11— Retreat into the Sudeten Mountains

On the road again we marched in splendid sunshine. Higher and higher into the mountains we climbed. It was difficult not to look back into the valley. In the distance we saw our home town; smoke rose from its center. Columns of dirt shot high into the sky. An artillery dual for dominance of my home had begun. Farther along the road we entered the dark pine forest so typical of the Sudeten Mountains. Branches were hung heavily laden with snow. Clouds of silvery snow dust, highlighted by rays of sunshine, filtered from the tops of gigantic firs. It was heavenly. Silence, only interrupted by the crunching of our boots in the snow. Around noon, we reached Landeshut. Again the local quartermaster assigned quarters. Ours was a mansion at the edge of town. We, and about ten other soldiers, had a wonderful butler who served us hand and foot; he was left behind to care for the residence — while his master had fled! Some of the soldiers told us that they had been with small units, surrounded and often twenty or more kilometers behind the Soviet lines. For some three weeks they had fought their way from the Polish-Soviet border toward friendly territory and finally were able to simply walk through both the Soviet and German lines. Some splinter groups had reorganized as independent battle elements and continued to fight until they were reunited with their divisions. I could not believe that I was in the middle of this chaos. I no longer felt the heroic defender of my home, only a terribly frightened boy. But I had survived. Everywhere along the route, but especially here in this town on the mountain pass into Czechoslovakia, we saw large posters that showed a beastly Soviet soldier mistreating a young German woman.

> Achtung, achtung. Das Oberkommando der Wehrmacht gibt bekannt.
> 16 February 1945. Our resistance in Lower Silesia has stiffened. The enemy could make only minimal advances. In counterattacks we forced the enemy to regroup.[8]

We were safe, but still we did not know what had happened to our parents. When we left Jauer there was much confusion all around us. We heard that Soviet tanks had penetrated far behind us and that at one time we were surrounded by the enemy — a terrible thought. Eventually our counterattacking forces broke the encirclement and destroyed the Soviet armor pincer. Apparently our parents were not on the route we had taken, so there was a good chance that Grandfather's *Trek* could have been overrun by the Soviets.

Lothar Scholz (*left*), the author's classmate and best friend, and the author, just before leaving for the front to serve as boy soldiers. *Author's collection.*

About a week later Mother and Tante Kläre came to Landeshut to purchase foodstuffs. From the quartermaster they heard that Lothar and I had survived and were living in splendor in a villa in one of the better parts of town. We were reunited with much joy and hugging. Mother told us that our families and the five wagons had barely escaped destruction by Soviet armor. The Soviet pincer closed only a few hundred yards behind their *Trek*. The wagons of other farmers were crushed by tanks that rolled over horses, wagons, and their precious cargo. Hundreds lost their lives, but our families had made it safely into the mountains. Lothar and I decided right there and then that, for a while at least, we would leave fighting the war to professionals.

The entire Thamm clan and Lothar's family were quartered in Altreichenau, a small farming village farther up in the Sudeten Mountains. Quarters were small and sparse, but warm. The quartermaster had, much to the frustration of the owners, taken the living room of each house and designated it "refugee quarters." Our large horses could barely squeeze into the stables built for their small mountain ponies. We had to unharness our horses outside, or they could not get through the low doorways. Lothar and I stayed a few days with our families, but living quarters were terribly crowded. Mother, Helga, Tante Kläre, her four children, and our poor old Preuss Oma — and now I — all lived in the farmer's living room. We slept on straw that we piled into a corner during the day. Mother and Tante Kläre cooked on the farmer's kitchen stove after the farmer's wife had finished her meals. André, the French prisoner of war who had driven Tante Kläre's wagon here, slept with his beloved horses in the stable. It was not an all-together great living arrangement. So, after some debate, Lothar and I left for the front. There was an added advantage for our folks: we left our ration cards with our families.

PART FOUR

Boy Soldiers

Chapter 12

Oh, to Be a Soldier

It was a decision based more on the economics of living space and rationed food than on patriotism. However, there may have been a bit of adventurism among the motives for leaving our families in that little village in the mountains. On a crisp morning Lothar and I walked from Altreichenau, through a narrow mountain pass to Bolkenhain. Large signs directed "stragglers" to report to the local *Kampfkommandant* whose offices were located at city hall. We assumed that we fell into the straggler category. We were just two of many local youths from areas overrun by the Soviets. Some were still filtering through the lines, others, like the two of us, came from locations this side of the Sudeten Mountains. The clerk at city hall told us to report to the training camp on the hill facing the old *Bolkoburg*, a fortress on top of the hill overlooking the little town. The fortress had looked defiantly into the lowlands since the twelfth century. Lothar and I were somewhat disillusioned. Somehow we had been under the impression that there was a dire need for fighters at the front. Combat Command Bolkenhain was of the opinion that we, and the many other boys, needed considerable training before being permitted to "play with the big boys."

Our training camp was on the site that had once been our Boy Scout campground, the place where I and many others had spent our summer youth training eons ago. Several hundred boys between the ages of fourteen and sixteen were already getting basic combat training. For the newly arrived there would be no laurels earned in combat with the dreaded enemy. Our first assignment was cleaning our barracks' interior, including the latrines, then we shoveled snow, tended the fires in the barracks' potbellied stoves, and cleaned several empty barracks. These housekeeping tasks kept us busy from early morning until late in the afternoon. It was not exactly what we had envisioned we would be doing so near the front line.

We were all early risers, whether we wanted to be or not. Military discipline was strict, there was no room for disagreement. Food was plain, but good. Breakfast consisted of black bread, an indefinable wartime fruit jam, and coffee made of roasted barley. There were always just a few moments after breakfast when life did indeed seem wonderful. Here on the hill we saw the sun touching the stubby tower of the *Bolkoburg* across town from our hilltop long before it lit up the narrow valley's houses and streets below us. Dinner, served at midday, was always the typical German Army stew or soup, and for the evening meal we again had black bread with, this time, a meat product called "sausage" and a good bottle of local beer. All in all, not bad chow for the fifth war year! We had another advantage here at Combat Command Bolkenhain: We became members of the German Army. For us boys especially, it was a great honor — and an adventure of sorts. In other sectors most of those between sixteen and sixty became part of the much-maligned *Volkssturm*, the home guard.

Chapter 13

Sergeant "One-Eye"

Finally it was our turn to be trained in the fine and ancient art of warfare. Early on a Monday morning, immediately after breakfast, an elderly soldier ordered us to fall out and get into platoon formations. Tallest boy at the right side of the formation, and then by height down the line to the shortest one. When he was satisfied with the arrangement, he told us to remember the spot we each were standing in and to never forget it. He told us that this would be our place in this platoon as long as we were here. He left us standing in the early morning freeze as he walked back into the warm orderly room.

We stood at attention until a haggard sergeant emerged from the orderly room. He walked toward us with a pronounced limp. Slowly and deliberately he viewed the platoon just as an auctioneer views prized cattle. "So," he growled, "you are Germany's last hope! Are you what the Greatest Field Marshal of All Times calls the saviors of the Fatherland?" He walked past us looking each boy in the first squad in the eyes. "Did you hear what I said?" He paused deliberately. "I asked a question. I am your sergeant. When I ask a question, I want to hear an answer." He screamed, "Do you hear me?"

Collectively we croaked, "Yes, Sergeant."

He screamed again, "I can't hear you."

We shouted in unison, "Yes, Sergeant."

Again, he screamed, "Well, let's see what the Führer's last hope of Fatherland defenders are made of." He limped to the center of the parade field and screamed, "Ten times around the field for the Führer. Double time!"

We started jogging in union toward the outer perimeter of the grounds.

"A little faster, gentlemen, the Führer wants to have his boys in good shape to defend the Fatherland."

We increased our pace.

"Faster, gentlemen!"

We again increased our pace. The formation started to stretch out. Some of the boys at the front faded and the formation began to disintegrate. Finally some of the boys, white clouds of breath expelling from lungs, could no longer keep up the fast pace of the rest, slowed down, and started to walk. In a flash and in spite of his shot-up leg, the sergeant rushed up and screamed sarcastically, "Is this what the Hitler Youth has produced? A bunch of weaklings? Move it! Move it! Move it! I'll drill you until the shit boils in your asshole. Do you hear me? Until the shit boils in your asshole. The Führer does not want weaklings! He wants Fatherland defenders! You are his last hope. Run!"

Then he leisurely returned to the center of the parade ground, lit a cigarette, and, with some apparent difficulty, folded his arms across his chest. He watched as we, heaving, coughing, struggled to make the last circuit around the parade ground our best round.

As we came out of the last turn the elderly soldier emerged from the orderly room. He surveyed the decrepit group and told us to get into formation just as he had told us a little while ago. He reminded us that we were not a bunch of sheep, but German soldiers, and never to forget it. As we struggled into formation he turned and walked toward the sergeant, saluted, and returned to the warmth of the orderly room. The sergeant looked at us in total disgust. He limped first one way then the other, his eyes roving — no, only one eye roved, the other looked straight ahead — across this group of miserable human beings. He walked totally around the platoon, returned to front and center, and spoke in an almost normal human voice. "I will make soldiers out of you! I will turn you into an efficient fighting machine. The German soldier is the toughest, the best, no, the only soldier in the world worth being called a soldier — and I will make soldiers out of you. You may think you are just a bunch of boys, but when I am through with you, you will be the most efficient killing machine the world has ever known — or you will be dead!" He paused. We all looked at him — we believed him. He stood there in the morning mist. His one eye looked straight ahead, the other roamed across this bunch of future soldiers. For unknown reasons his entire body tilted somewhat to the left. He stood there, in his field uniform, a fascinating, almost mythical figure. In the buttonhole of his tunic was the black, white, and red ribbon of the Iron Cross Second Class; at the center of his left pocket glittered the black and silver Iron Cross First Class; slightly below and to the left was the oval ring of silver oak leaves crossed diagonally by a rifle, the Infantry Combat Badge; below that the Wounded Medal in Silver, signifying a major combat wound; and above the elbow of his right arm were two silver tank insignias identifying the bearer as an expert close-combat tank killer.

Only when Sergeant One-Eye was satisfied that we could withstand the physical rigors of frontline duty did the fun stuff finally start: We went to the firing range. All those already familiar with the standard prewar rifle, the 7.92-mm Mauser 98K, were introduced to the Sturmgewehr MP-43 assault rifle, the MP-38 machine-pistol, the Soviet PPSh41 "burp gun," and, of course, the famous *Panzerfaust*.[1] We did not get to fire the rifles and machine pistols as much as we wanted — there was a shortage of ammunition at the training camp. However, we had sufficient *Panzerfaust* ammunition at hand. We fired the *Panzerfaust* at trees which the newly arriving stragglers cut up into firewood; there was enough firewood to last for many months. Sergeant One-Eye said, "Get to know the PPSh well, you never know when you'll get hold of one. It's a damn good weapon!" After less than two weeks under the harsh tutelage of Sergeant One-Eye, we were sufficiently trained, he thought, to guide patrols into the area where we had grown up. Maybe not trained to hold our own in fierce combat, but enough to serve as armed guides — scouts.

At our last briefing the elderly soldier who was Sergeant One-Eye's subordinate informed us that among the many German elements virtually annihilated was the 100th Jäger (Light Infantry) Division. Elements of that division had fought a desperate delaying action. Under constant pressure from overwhelming Soviet forces the remnants of the division had retreated rapidly through Poland, crossed the Oder River, and then, still fighting on all sides, had retreated into Lower Silesia and toward the Sudeten Mountains. Much of the division's artillery and its logistic train, along with all situation maps, had been lost. Who would have ever thought there would be a need for tactical maps for the foothills of the Sudeten Mountains? Without maps and local guides one of the division's supporting tank battalions had gotten lost on the Autobahn, Germany's superhighway. Under attack from the north, west, and east the battalions selected a route that led directly into a Soviet column advancing on the Autobahn in the other direction. Soft, marshy soil on both sides of the road made evasion for either faction impossible. Here occurred one of those actions for which there are no training manuals. Firing from all barrels the battalion raced for the next exit road leading south toward the mountains. Remnants of the battalion eventually returned to German lines. The elderly soldier told us that until tactical maps for these areas became available local commanders all along the Eastern Front were forced to rely on native guides. This would be our main job.

Here at the training camp were numerous boys, fifteen- and sixteen-year-olds, more than willing to serve "their" army in any capacity. They had already lost their homes and everything dear to them to the attacking Soviets. Many hungered for revenge — or just adventure — but most important was that they were thoroughly familiar with the army's operational area — the boys' home turf. The elderly soldier wondered aloud how good we would be as scouts and guides.

Chapter 14

Frontline Duty

Shortly after breakfast we assembled in front of our barracks. We stood around filled with excitement waiting for the trucks that would take us near the front line. We were the chosen ones. Others, who had reported to the training camp while Sergeant One-Eye had us under his strict tutelage, looked enviously at our weapons, our field packs, and our camouflaged winter-white uniforms. We tried to act nonchalant, but could not totally hide our pride for having passed Sergeant One-Eye's muster. The trucks arrived and we mounted with much ado. From the edge of the forest we walked the last two miles to our assigned sector. We arrived at the front line with some of the replacements that Combat Command Bolkenhain had managed to scrape up. The platoon leader, a haggard-looking corporal, wore an incredibly clean, well-pressed uniform with the Iron Cross First Class on the left front pocket of his tunic, the Close Combat above the pocket, and the black Wounded Medal below the Iron Cross; his upper left sleeve glittered with an assortment of the much-coveted tank-killer badges. The corporal's boots were spit-shined.

"I am Corporal Schwertfeger. You are in Combat Sector Jauer." He pointed to one of the men. "Pfc Burkhard will assign you to your new homes. He will show you your combat position, the spot you will defend until you die or until I tell you to vacate it. He will also show you where your forward lookout station will be." Without another glance at the sorry huddle of soldiers he turned and said over his shoulder, "Carry on," as he walked away slightly limping to one of the cottages. Lothar whispered in my ear, "A carbon copy of Sergeant One-Eye, but at least he still has two eyes."

Chapter 14 — Frontline Duty

Pfc Burkhard quickly led us to our squad bunkers. They were not really what I thought bunkers would be, having watched newsreels of the elaborate ones on the Siegfried and the Atlantic Wall lines. What we had here were peasant cottages that had been somewhat crudely fortified. All were near the edge of the village positioned along the cemetery wall. We saw that logs with cut-in firing ports at shoulder height protected the already small windows. Every outside door had vertical tree trunks rammed into the ground — they prevented direct access. Each of these barriers had a firing port. The tree trunk barriers also served to deflect light to help with the blackout.

Pfc Burkhard assigned Lothar and me to one of the cottages. The inside was dank and musty, but two bare lightbulbs gave sufficient light — yes, as incredible as this may sound, electric power was still functioning here. However, it was a far cry from the already sparse accommodations at the training camp. There was little ventilation. The "aroma" of body odor, leather, gun oil, and the combination of wood-fire and tobacco smoke permeated our new home. Inside wooden planks, propped up with heavy timbers, strengthened the ceilings of the cottages. Each of the small rooms had two-tiered bunks, actually rectangular wooden boxes filled with straw covered with blankets. There were two empty boxes; those were Lothar's and mine. He selected the lower one, I the upper. Pfc Burkhard ordered us to get fresh straw from the barn, fill the boxes, and grab two of the familiar scratchy, gray woolen army field blankets. He indicated that this would be our home until we got relieved. The latrine was in back in the former pigsty. Water, even hot water, was in the kitchen. All the comforts of home.

Lothar was in total shock, and I was not too far behind him. After Pfc Burkhard left to show the others to their "homes" he said, "They must be kidding. How can anyone live like this? How many live in this dump?" We counted bunks. Ten in the first room. We looked into the only other room of the cottage. Lothar said under his breath, "Good God, twelve in the other room! Twenty-two people in a place built to house three or four. That's incredible." We looked into the farm's kitchen: big table in the middle, a large shaded lamp above. Army mess gear filled the cupboards, a small fire crackled in the large wood-burning stove, and a huge cauldron with hot water sizzled on the rear of the stove — comfortable. "This looks a hell of a lot better than the other two rooms," said Lothar.

Opposite: A corner of a frontline village. ***Author's diary.***

"Let's look at the latrine." The only other door from the kitchen did indeed lead to the pigsty. Lothar opened it, looked, and immediately shut the door. "My God, do people live like that?" Curious, I pushed past him and entered the pigsty. Obviously, there were no pigs stabled here any longer, but the stench had not faded. Along one side of the sty was a one-holer that had been moved several times. Exposed and covered with lime were three mounds of excrement — frozen. The farmer's "toilet" had served maybe three or four people during its better days. With twenty-two adults it was entirely too small — thus the piles of disgust covered with lime. For Lothar and I, city-bred and used to flush toilets, this was the real wake-up call. "I don't mind dying for the Fatherland, but I can never go to the bathroom here," Lothar said emphatically. He had thought the communal latrine at the training camp was bad, but this? I agreed, but did not know what choice we had. Neither did Lothar. After a while he said, "And just think, we could be with the folks back up in the mountains." I almost agreed with him, but thought that those toilets up there were not exactly great either. Lothar agreed reluctantly.

We had thrown our backpacks on the bunks, hung weapons and ammo pouches on the bedpost mimicking the arrangements of other bunks. Now we went out and searched for the barn to get straw. Others were already there grabbing small bales and carrying them to their abodes. No one, except maybe a small fellow everyone called Little Erich, looked very happy. We guessed their accommodations were not much better than ours. Lothar and I grabbed one of the bales — one should be enough. We filled the two wooden boxes, our beds, with the straw and stretched over each bunk one of the army blankets. I told Lothar that I hated sleeping on straw just like the cows we had in our stable. He just nodded his head.

In our small sector the farm and cemetery walls, stone barns, and farmers' houses were turned into fortified positions. We had machine guns in holes broken through the walls. Sandbags placed overhead on wooden racks protected gunners from artillery shrapnel. Designated fields of fire covered the entire meadow — my grandfather's former haying field — south of the Wütende Neisse River. For the boys from Jauer the first glance at their Soviet-occupied home town was at best foreboding. From this vantage point we easily saw the steeples of Jauer's churches, the *Piasten* castle, and city hall. We also had a clear view of all buildings along the southern edge of town, especially a farm that belonged to one of Grandfather's friends. A small part of Jauer, the eastern end, toward our right flank, was actually still in German hands.

Some of the new arrivals immediately bonded with the other platoon members — they had recovered from wounds and returned to the front. Two of the new guys, still wearing bandages, had "deserted" to the front from the rear area hospital. The rest of the new arrivals stood aside, somewhat uncomfortable. The veterans called them "the Dregs." The Dregs were the ones who had avoided frontline duty until this very last moment. While the veterans had fought six long years for the Fatherland, some of these Nazi party members had occupied "positions essential to the war effort" throughout the war. The veterans saw a bunch of misfits who had dodged frontline duty for many years, and some brats in ill-fitting uniforms clutching a variety of deadly weapons. At first glance they looked at us boys as a useless inconvenience.

The Dregs soon stood guard duty, while the boy soldiers pitched in with all the menial chores such as cleaning the bunkers, carrying ammunition to the machine gun positions, and carrying aluminum thermos canister backpacks from the rear field kitchen to the line. We enjoyed cleaning the guns and being useful in many other ways. We knew that once we became acclimatized to frontline service we would start guiding patrols through the neighborhoods we knew so well.

There was one of the Dregs who never complained — Little Erich. Today one would say Little Erich was "short one brick of a load." Throughout the past six war years Little Erich had not been deemed suitable for military service because of his limited mental capacity. However, in these perilous times he was called to serve his country. Little Erich wore his uniform proudly. During R&R (rest and recuperation) in Bolkenhain he asked anyone with a camera to take his photo. Little Erich was incredibly strong. When it was time to refortify our positions he carried two forty-pound sacks of sand some 400 yards from a builder's yard to the line. All the others had problems with one of the sacks. He was so enthusiastic every once in a while Corporal Schwertfeger forced Little Erich to take a break, something entirely against the corporal's nature. No matter where he went, Little Erich always had his rifle slung over his chest even while carrying the heaviest loads.

Little Erich was a scrounger; the folks who had fled this village had left behind plenty of firewood, fruit preserves, pickled eggs, and smoked meat and sausage. Little Erich scurried through the houses, the basements, and the storage sheds and found eatables to keep us well fed and comfortable. He scampered through the village and found firewood, brought it to the platoon area, chopped it, and piled it in neat stacks in the shed behind our bunker. During one of his forays he discovered preserved fruit in large glass jars. In the evening he proudly displayed his find while dividing it in equal shares for everyone. His beaming enthusiasm was infectious. He was like a little mouse scurrying around, collecting morsels for the coming hard winter. Everyone, even the Dregs, looked at Little Erich as a welcome addition to the platoon. One morning he came through the backyards lugging a huge earthen jar. We saw him laboring through a nearby broken fence, his rifle this time slung over his back, banging against his butt. He had a wide grin on his face.

"Hey, Little Erich," one of the guys shouted, "what have you there this time?"

"Pickled eggs," he answered. "Pickled eggs. Hundreds of pickled eggs." He had found them in the basement of the farm next door. He laughed, "They'll make good eating tonight." Everyone just loved Little Erich.

Unlike most of the other Dregs, we boy soldiers never complained and soon the old-timers accepted us, and Little Erich, as at least somewhat useful entities. A few days after we arrived at the line Corporal Schwertfeger brought us to the outpost line for terrain familiarization. We listened respectfully as he explained in excruciating detail the area before us. He then asked a few questions and finally realized that we knew the area under Soviet control better than he. He then questioned us on good covert approaches to the town and the nearby villages. We proudly told him all the various ways we had explored the crevices of our town in every detail. After a while he started to laugh and said, "Enough, enough. I can tell you know that area better than I." He then told us to pay good attention. There was something that he knew better than we — the minefield in front of our line, and the Russian one in front of their line. One wrong step, he cautioned, and we would be history.

Tonight we would go to the dairy to get what butter is left. Our point man would guide us you through our minefield. Then one or two of us would lead the way to the back gate of the dairy. He pointed to the right of our position at two black and white rods, the entrance to the mine-free alley. We all looked anxiously in the direction of the rods. The alley was only three feet wide, which may seem like a lot, but in the dark of night it seems a lot narrower. He hesitated, then cautioned us to be especially careful at night because those rods were almost impossible to see. Coming back from the Soviet side we should not be overanxious to get back, we should follow the point man and walk in his footprints. He shifted his weight and pointed where the Russian mine-free alley was some 1,500 meters directly opposite our front. We should watch that sector closely. He turned to one of the Dregs, "Hey soldier, I don't want you to screw up when the boys lead us to the butter. You keep a sharp lookout and if one of them Ruskies comes through that alley you had better spot him and tell one of my lads." He turned his attention back to us and mentioned that those Ruskies also knew where the butter was, and that they like it just as much as we. He looked in the direction of the Dregs, I don't want to run into a Ruskie butter patrol. Understood?" The Dregs looked uncomfortable. They already envied the good relationship between the boys and the old-timers.

> Achtung, achtung. Das Oberkommando
> der Wehrmacht gibt bekannt.
>
> 24 April 1945. Effective attack against his rear area supply lines forced the enemy to pull back his armor point from the Dresden area. Fortress Bautzen defended itself courageously against heavy attacks.[1]

Guiding troops became the boy soldier's primary mission, the secondary one, a mission far more rewarding than the first, was bringing stragglers and civilians out of Soviet territory into our lines. During the turmoil of the retreat from the eastern border of Poland into Silesia Soviet armor had bypassed thousands of our soldiers. It was the job of Soviet infantry to either capture or kill whatever German troops had been overrun. Large and small elements, as well as individual soldiers, attempted to elude the Soviets or fight their way back into German-held territory. Almost nightly one or two soldiers, who had been overrun a month ago and worked their way through the Soviet lines, would arrive at our position and tell us about groups of soldiers or civilians hidden behind Soviet lines. Since the OKW had never contemplated fighting on German soil, it had neither maps in its inventory nor any knowledge of the local area. Many local boys were only too eager to help. We guided patrols through villages and towns where we had grown up, where we had gone to school, where we had played children's games. The night following the request for help one or two boy soldiers would guide a small patrol into that area to rescue those groups. These were probably the most gratifying patrols we ever made.

> General Brückner wrote in *History of the Rhine-Westphalian 6th Infantry Division, 1939–1945* that "some twelve 14-year-old boys, whose homes were occupied by the Soviets, asked to become members of my battalion. They refused to leave, so I had them put into uniforms and assigned to reconnaissance patrols. With their knowledge of the local area we produced reconnaissance results not before possible. During one Soviet armored assault these boys, who had barely become acquainted with the Panzerfaust, destroyed several Stalin (heavy) and T-34 (medium) tanks. Encircled during a Soviet counterattack, they defended their position for several hours until relieved by my counterattack."[2]

Our Main Line of Resistance was also our outpost line. In fact, it was our only line. To our rear were some ten miles of a narrow country road that soon became steep, serpentine mountain road. Short on troops, this area was No-Man's Land patrolled by fierce-looking, heavily armed Croatian volunteers dressed in SS uniforms. They were strange men. They sported heavy black beards, rode small, tough mountain ponies, and shot, without questions, any Soviet found behind German lines. Their mules carried machine guns and ammunition boxes in packsaddles. The mules walked tethered behind the ponies. Every so often a Soviet combat patrol went undetected through our thinly manned line to raise havoc in our rear area. The Croatians made sure that this usually was the Soviets' last patrol.

Although I was in the backwaters of the great offensive that would shortly destroy the Fatherland, to a novice fifteen-year-old boy soldier, the fighting in our sector appeared furious — and terribly exciting! Almost every night one or two boys would lead a combat patrol through the back alleys and hollows of what had once been our homes. There were few bitter battles along our front line — only skirmishes. Initially we conducted missions called "Russian grabbers," i.e. patrols would surprise a Soviet sentry, subdue him, and bring him back for interrogation. This practice was abandoned when interrogators found that the Soviet sentries knew little. Some did not even know they were on German soil — most had no concept of geography. The first map they had ever seen was the interrogator's. During most of these forays no shots were ever fired. Only infrequently did German and Soviet patrols meet. More often than not both sides tried to avoid contact. If contact was unavoidable, after a short, heavy firefight, the disadvantaged party withdrew hastily.

Lothar and I had been in the forward position a week or two. In a few days we were to be relieved. We looked forward to a hot shower, delousing, and clean uniforms. Early that morning several artillery rounds impacted in our area. There was much shouting and rushing around as everyone quickly grabbed warm clothing, guns, and ammunition and rushed out of the bunkers. Lothar and I were the last to emerge. Small arms fire was all around us, bright white flares rose in the sky. We heard the heavy sound of a diesel engine as the *Vierling*, a quadruple 20-mm antiaircraft gun on half-tracks, came out of its hiding place in the barn. Men scrambled aboard as the machine rumbled past us into position behind the cemetery wall, belching stinking diesel smoke. Even before we reached our position at the stone wall, the four barrels of the *Vierling* started to throw a hail of explosive shells into the attacking Soviets. Four or five machine guns in the cemetery wall fired short bursts. Lothar and I started firing. Empty shell casings flew everywhere. There was smoke, flashes of light, collapsing figures bleeding in the snow. The entire scene seemed unreal; it seemed to vibrate in front of us. Just as suddenly as it began the attack came to an abrupt halt as the Soviets ran out of troops. The snow was black and red from powder, smoke, and blood. Where just moments ago there had been incredible noise, now there was silence. No one had given the command to cease firing; seasoned troops knew when it was all over. They left the few retreating Russians dragging their dead and wounded back to their position — but the stench of cordite and the smoke lingered on.

In this eerie silence we heard someone sobbing, whimpering. At first our corporal walked angrily along the line. He found Little Erich, curled up in a fetal position, shaking like a leaf. The corporal looked around, embarrassed, uncomfortable, then cradled Little Erich in his arms. We heard him whisper, "Don't worry, Little Erich, we won't let anything happen to you. We'll take care of you."

After some uncomfortable moments Little Erich calmed down and the corporal and he rose, both terribly embarrassed, from the hole where Little Erich had hidden.

"I don't want anyone to ever mention this to Little Erich or to anyone else, understand!"

It was not a question. For a brief moment we had seen the corporal's human side, and he did not like it.

From the farmhouse to our rear the cook carried hot coffee in a large thermos backpack. He filled our canteens, and his helper topped it off with a shot of cognac. I held my canteen in both of my uncontrollably shaking hands. Hot coffee splashed in my lap and severely burned both my thighs and my private parts. No one laughed! After-action shock. I guess, sooner or later, it can happen to anyone.

Two days after the attack fresh troops relieved us and we first walked through the farmlands into the woods, then rode trucks to the training and rest camp on the hill overlooking the charming little town of Bolkenhain. Sergeant One-Eye watched our arrival. He invited Corporal Schwertfeger into his barracks. We went to the shower facilities, threw our uniforms onto a large pile, washed our filthy bodies, were deloused, and received clean uniforms.

We were only a day or two at the camp when Sergeant One-Eye called "his lads" together. He told us how proud he was that we had served well. Then he told us of civil government plans to clear the rear area of all refugees. If we had family located in the mountains, he said, we should help them move through the pass into Czechoslovakia, and then return to Bolkenhain.

Lothar, I, and several other boy soldiers opted for that assignment. We hitched a ride on a supply truck to Altreichenau. Our families were all ready to depart. We helped load the wagons, harnessed the horses, and departed rather gladly from that austere mountain village. Our family's *Trek* eventually stopped at the quaint little village of Altenbuchen, just outside the city of Trautenau, then in the Sudetenland, part of former Czechoslovakia. Here, protected by the Sudeten Mountains from the harsh northerly winds the weather was very pleasant. The fields had already turned green. Spring was in the air, and Lothar and I soon forgot the rigors of frontline service. But, we felt the Fatherland needed everyone on the other side of the mountains.

Lothar and I arrived at Landeshut during the early afternoon. We waited in the great hall of the railroad station until the train, a combination passenger and freight, left for the front. It was still frosty in the mountains; snow covered the passes. The air was crisp as the supply train slowly passed in total blackout through the gap in the Sudeten Mountains from Landeshut to Bolkenhain. Rail traffic between Landeshut and Bolkenhain was possible only during hours of darkness because a portion of the route was within Soviet artillery range, but what a beautiful night it was. From tiny villages in deep valleys the evening church bells called all believers to prayer. The crisp snow on the huge firs glittered like cold, blue diamonds. As we rounded the last turn through the high mountain pass a panoramic view opened. From our vantage point we watched, each lost in his private thoughts. Dark pine forests spread their protective arms over the land. Smoke rose from chimneys of thatch-roofed cottages in small, storybook villages. Far into the lowland were the fields and meadows of our farms. This is what all of those on this train were fighting for. Some twelve miles away flares lit the sky; infrequently strings of tracers arched silently into the night like bright cotton balls; they appeared to float into nowhere and then disappeared suddenly. Faraway, near the horizon was my home.

As Soviet forces of the 1st Ukrainian Front continued their westward drive, Combat Sector Jauer saw only sporadic small unit actions. Almost every night our combat patrols probed their line, and theirs probed ours. Occasionally stragglers still came through the Soviet lines into our area. Some stragglers reported pockets of refugees and soldiers hidden behind enemy lines. It was our mission to rescue them. These were always the most dangerous, yet also the most rewarding patrols. Time was of the essence. Most often the stragglers were too exhausted to lead the patrol back behind enemy lines. From detailed descriptions several boys drew a map of the area of interest. Then we debated the best way of entry and exit. On one occasion we found three women, two with whining infants. To quiet them the mothers taped the babies' mouths shut. We were afraid it might kill the children, but had no choice. At night the slightest noise carries far. Two of the soldiers carried the babies, their mothers too exhausted to do so. Fortunately, luck was with us; all came through this ordeal unharmed.

The mountainous terrain south of Jauer was the type easily defended by infantry armed with our hallelujah antitank weapon. Soviet strength lay in their many tanks; the mountains favored us, the riflemen. Tanks had great difficulty traversing this terrain. The narrow valleys forced them to stay on the road, where they became easy targets. The narrow meadows were mined and the roads barricaded with tree trunk "tank traps." With time the road from the front line into the mountains had become heavily fortified. Engineering troops, assisted by local laborers and foreign workers, constructed huge tank barriers out of large pine trunks in areas where the road squeezed through cliffs or narrows. The barriers had an opening just wide enough to permit a large tank to pass. In a cradle above the barrier were other tree trunks held in position by ropes. Should an enemy attempt to pass, the guard — and there was always an armed guard at every barrier — cut the rope and the tree trunks rolled from the cradle and jammed into the slots of the barrier. It took considerable effort by many men to lift the tree trunks from their jammed position and hoist them back to the elevated position above the barrier. I learned how difficult that was when we had to raise these logs after we repelled a Soviet attack in March. The whole area some distance from the barrier had cleared field of fire, well-constructed fox holes, and all sorts of fake defensive positions that would draw the enemy's fire.

Standing guard in our machine gun positions at night was an eerie experience. The view was spectacular. With total darkness the stars became ever more brilliant. There were none of the ambient noises of a farm village — no hogs grunting into their troughs, no horses snorting in their stalls, no cows mooing in the stables, and no guard dogs howling into the night. It was quiet except for the occasional weapon clinking against a stone, or the whispers between guards. I and another boy stood watch one particular night as the full moon climbed over the horizon and illuminated the valley. Some 200 yards away a row of stubby willow trees grew along a shallow creek. Every few years basket weavers had trimmed young branches from those trees for basket weaving material. The new growth of thin branches, illuminated by the cold moonlight with the light cover of snow in the background, gave those dark brown willow trees a near-human appearance — like crouching men wearing large fur caps. Only the occasional clink of metal against metal, when someone shifted the barrel of a machine gun, interrupted the night's silence. Intermittently, far to the north, a white flare momentarily cast its brilliant flicker of light and shadow across the snow. Intensely we, one with his field glasses, searched each sector in front of our position. Just as Corporal Schwertfeger had taught us we searched and stopped, searched again, and then retraced our search pattern. I nudged the boy with the binoculars. Pointing toward the creek I asked, "Is there movement?"

"Where?"

"Right there, at the creek!"

"I don't know."

"Look again!" We concentrated our attention on the creek, the willows, and the area beyond. Indeed, there seemed to be someone moving among the willow trees.

"Did you see that?"

"Seems to be more than one."

"Over there to the right."

"Call a challenge!"

One of us shouted very loud, "Who goes there?" Silence.

Again, "Who goes there?" More silence.

"I think I see the glint of a gun."

"Where?"

"Over to the left. Must be a whole bunch."

I ran to the neighboring gun position. "We think there is a Russian patrol at the creek. Take a look!"

The other boy shifted the machine gun in the direction of the creek, aimed at the row of willow trees. As I returned to my position I threw myself next to the gun and lifted the ammunition belt. A short burst. Every fifth round a tracer. The tracers arched like lazy cotton balls toward the grove of trees. To our right a parachute flare climbed into the sky and white tracer rounds from a second machine gun slammed into the trees. Another machine gun entered the fracas. Three kilometers to the north, from the Russian side, several flares burst into the night sky. Behind us doors slammed. The sound of heavy boots in the snow. It was Corporal Schwertfeger. He and others came running toward the cemetery wall.

"What in hell is going on?"

One of us shouted, "Russian patrol at the creek."

"Where?"

"Right down there at the creek."

Corporal Schwertfeger grabbed the glasses and studied the area carefully, then shouted, "Cease fire! Cease fire, Goddamn it, cease fire!"

Slowly the firing stopped. Now flares rose into the sky only from the Russian side, and after a few minutes, it was all quiet again. Corporal Schwertfeger was mad. His sleep had been interrupted. He stood there without his heavy winter coat. Not only was he mad, he was freezing.

"Who started this fracas?" he shouted. "I want to know who started all this pissy shooting?"

We admitted that we probably were the guilty culprits. "We thought that there was a patrol in those trees, and when there was no answer to the challenge, we opened fire."

"You nitwits, trees don't answer your challenge. They don't answer to nothing. They just stand there."

"But, but, but ..."

"But, nothing. You boys can't be trusted with anything, not even standing guard." As some of the others gathered, he relented. "Well, I guess it could happen to anyone. The harder you look at those damned willow trees the more they look as if they move — and I guess at night those basket weaver willows can look like Russians with fur caps. Better safe than sorry." He turned. "I am going back to bed, and I don't want to hear another shot unless it comes from the other side! Do you hear me?"

Embarrassed, we said dutifully and in unison, "Yes, Sir, Corporal," and for the rest of the night all was quiet.

The next morning Corporal Schwertfeger reported to headquarters: At 0345 hours an attempt by Soviet reconnaissance patrol to pierce our line was repulsed.

And we got an extra ration of brandy.

Chapter 15

The "Forgotten Front"

A railroad line snaked a few miles behind our line from the Upper Silesian anthracite coal field near the old Polish border along the northern edge of the Sudeten Mountains to the armament industries in the western part of Germany. I would not learn until many years later that the defense of this line along the southern Soviet flank was of utmost strategic importance to the Reich. There was a concerted effort to keep this rail line open. Silesian miners dug coal until May 1945, and the railroaders carried that coal westward. Passenger trains rolled as scheduled, even on 9 May 1945 — the day of surrender. Since there were few furious engagements between Soviet and Germans along the line, this front became known as the "Forgotten Front."

Statistics simply cannot tell the whole story. Statistics can only tell the German railroad employees' accomplishments. While the ground above them was often raked by Soviet artillery fire, the coal miners added some 6–8,000 tons of coal daily to existing reserves. Six coal trains, carrying 6–8,000 tons, left the Rybniker mines each night until the Soviets captured this area at the end of March; twelve coal trains, carrying some 16,000 tons, left the Karwinter mines each night until the 8th of May, one day before Germany capitulated. The railroaders also brought 1.7 million refugees into western Germany. On the return trip the trains carried food, ammunition, and fuel to the troops manning the "Forgotten Front." Other railroad operations consisted of shifting troops and armor from one sector to another, and, it seems almost ludicrous, the German Reichsbahn operated regularly scheduled commercial freight and passenger traffic until the very last day of the war.

The "Forgotten Front" was defended by remnants of German Army and Luftwaffe elements and elements of the 20th Estonian Infantry Division, supported by an assortment of old men and young boys, a medley of anti–Communist Croats, Ukrainians, Serbs, and Turks in German uniforms. As the Reich collapsed, city fortresses such as Glogau capitulated on the 1st of April 1945; the Americans and Soviets met at Torgau-on-the-Elbe on the 24th of April; Hitler committed suicide in his Berlin bunker on the 2nd of May; and after long months of bitter fighting the fortress city Breslau, the capital of Lower Silesia, capitulated on the 6th of May. But one fourth of Lower Silesia, defended by troops at the Forgotten Front, remained in German hands until after Germany capitulated on the 9th of May 1945.

Slowly the veterans at the Forgotten Front accepted boy soldiers as part of their combat team. Certainly we had more energy than the battle-weary men. Thus, we endeared ourselves by performing all sorts of menial chores such as cleaning the bunkers and hauling ammunition and supplies. Little Erich, the only one of the adults recently called to duty, worked with the boy soldiers and soon became the unit's mascot. There were still the Dregs who somehow never seemed to fit in. While we were at the front the Dregs pulled guard duty, but Corporal Schwertfeger would not allow them to go on patrols — he simply did not trust them.

Lothar and I and the other boy soldiers had become accustomed to living in the bunkers, sleeping during the day, and patrolling at night. We had penetrated the Soviet line several times — most often to rescue civilians and soldiers hidden in the basements of burned-out houses. We had never encountered any Soviets, rarely fired a shot, never had a person wounded or killed by landmines, because Corporal Schwertfeger, based on debriefing the stragglers and considering the boy soldiers' advice, always routed our paths carefully through unfriendly territory.

There are so many things the frontline soldier is never told. Like the others, my classmate and I had absolutely no idea what was going on outside of what we could see and hear. We did not hear news reports on the radio. There were no newspapers to be had. As far as we knew, the ordinary soldier had no concept of where the front line was; even if he cared, he probably had not the slightest idea what even the most general situation was. Here at the front line it was actually far calmer than at Bolkenhain. There we saw a kind of controlled chaos. Trucks towing artillery pieces crisscrossed the little town of Bolkenhain. Troops, heavily laden with gear, weapons, and ammunition marched in single file along the only road leading into the lowlands. Engineering troops, assisted by any person, man or woman, capable of handling a pick and shovel, were busy erecting huge tank barriers out of tree trunks which they rammed vertically into the ground; they then filled the inside of the barrier with stone and gravel. Engineers tied explosives with detonators and primer-cords onto large trees; long ago they had mined all the bridges, tunnels, and rocky cliffs overhanging the road leading northward, toward the front.

Some time ago the call had gone out that the army was badly in need of bicycles. The civilian population, long without a chance to buy anything, brought bicycles of many types for their lads to use against the Soviets. With a sufficient number of bicycles at hand the combat command organized many of the boys and experienced soldiers into "quick-reaction mobile tank hunter teams." Deployment of these tank hunter teams was actually quite effective. In this mountainous terrain they moved almost as well as motorized units, and in most instances they could penetrate large wooded areas faster than any motor vehicle. The Soviets had great difficulty spotting and firing on them, and bicycle patrols were not limited by the lack of scarce gasoline.

During intermittent stays at the Bolkenhain camp for rest, cleanup, and delousing, Sergeant One-Eye and one of his corporals taught infantry tactics, especially antitank destroyer techniques, to the boy soldiers. "Boys," he said. "Boys, war produces situations that neither the GEFAZ, nor I, nor Germany's best training manuals can describe. Nothing I can do will prepare you for the sheer terror that grips not only the novice, but everyone — at least every sane soldier, when he first sees the swift, ruthless attack by Soviet T-34s." The other veterans nodded in agreement. "All too often the rifleman stands alone. He will hear of the great support that headquarters promises, all bullshit! Propaganda from those 'Gold Pheasants'[1] in Berlin, nothing but plain bullshit." By now the boys were getting used to having Nazi party officials openly called that derogatory name. "Look around you," Sergeant One-Eye continued, "most of the brownshirts have vanished."

"But," one of the corporals, who had his empty left sleeve tucked under his belt, interrupted, "we have a few here in the 'ear, eye, and stomach' detachments who have managed to avoid duty to the Fatherland for more than five years."

At this stage of the war many men previously thought to be not fit for military service were drafted into ear, eye, & stomach platoons.

Soldiers hard of hearing and those with poor eyesight were matched to compensate for each other's shortcomings. "One ear and one eye soldier, over here" was the order. The one who could not see would tell the one who could not hear. Assigned to "stomach" platoons were those with ulcers or other digestive problems; they received special dietary rations and stood guard, went on patrols; all would do their bit for the Fatherland. Many a shirker with a friendly doctor's chit, who had thought he had escaped the harshness of military service ended up in one of these strange units. All in keeping with the Führer's last Order of the Day to his Eastern Front armies: "No one is too good to die for the Fatherland. Attack!" That order also included Hitler's edict that "He who gives the order to retreat is to be shot on the spot." The corporal continued, "We remind them of the Führer's edict and they don't like it one bit."

With a chuckle Sergeant One-Eye added, "As if we care!" Again grunts of approval from the seasoned veterans. "I have orders," he continued, "to shoot any bastards running away. This time around they too can become cannon fodder for the Führer."

The boys at the training camp had already seen the total confusion, the disorientation, and the chaos of war at ground level. They had been cut off from all friendly forces; their artillery support had been at best sporadic, and heavy machine gun fire from Soviet T-34 tanks allowed only the most foolhardy to launch their antitank missiles. They had heard from the boys at Siegersdorf that help had been a million miles away, but foolhardy or not, they survived, because they had an effective antitank weapon they had fired several times, a weapon they trusted. The "old" soldiers reminded us that when on your own, the Panzerfaust was indeed your hallelujah weapon.

Later, we wondered aloud about the sergeant's anti–Nazi remarks, but one of the veterans sneered, "What can they do to us? Send us to the Eastern Front?"

We were to remember the words of Sergeant One-Eye and the others. Those of us who survived would always remember the utter ruthlessness of those iron monsters. The noise, the roaring diesel engines, the clanking tracks, the sharp reports of the main gun, and the incessant bursts from machine guns were mind destroying. At times the tanks too seemed to be confused. They roared first one way, then another, they fired first on one target, then another, but always on any suspicious movement or obstacle, on any place where one could conceivably hide. We learned that reconnaissance by fire, engine and track noises, smoke, dust, and speed were a tanker's allies. However, to experienced soldiers reconnaissance by fire also meant the tanker was unsure of his target, and that the rifleman had only to lie in wait for the tank to come into killing range. To most of us the psychological impact of a swift, ruthless attack by tanks was almost unbearable terror. At times it even drove experienced combat veterans insane. Some would inexplicably launch more than one Panzerfaust, thus exposing their position to tank fire, others would spring from their concealed positions to run toward the rear only to become easy targets for any tank gunner.

We learned the truism "anything that can go wrong will go wrong." During an early morning Soviet assault in March 1945 one of their attack columns pierced our right flank. As happened so often in the confusion, our sector was neither notified nor ordered to pull back. Only when we heard the battle noise shifting from frontal firing to small arms fire and heavy explosions toward our right flank and rear did we realize that we were in danger of being cut off and surrounded. Corporal Schwertfeger sent a runner to the unit on our left to let them know that we were pulling back to avoid capture. We retreated, fighting on all sides, toward higher ground.

The total confusion of this type of walking encirclement is difficult to describe. Wireless communication was sporadic, artillery support fire nonexistent, air support not available. All things considered, the tactics used in the walking encirclement were relatively simple. Our forward element cleared the way southward. The rear guard slowed down the aggressively pursuing Soviet tank element, and our neighboring units bent their front from facing northward to facing toward the east. Foxholes (actually short trenches with an escape trench) had been dug some weeks ago by local construction troops, the same folks who had constructed the tank barriers, mined the bridges, and tied explosives to large trees that would become obstacles. The foxhole trenches were different from the usual ones: They had no breastworks or earthen mounds that could betray their location. All the earth was distributed elsewhere and covered with snow. These foxholes were almost invisible to the attacker. All trenches were placed to make quick escape into low cover, depressions, cliffs, or houses possible. Three men or boys occupied each position. Two to "dust off" the tank and accompanying infantry with automatic weapons fire, the third to fire the antitank weapon.

On that morning the process repeated itself twice or thrice. At each tank barrier we pulled the rope that had held back the tree trunks stored above the tank trap; they dropped into the barrier cradle and effectively blocked the road. Then came the torturous wait for the assault. The first tank to spot the barrier fired one or two rounds; the infantry quickly dismounted and deployed. We could not return fire because the tanks were beyond the range of our weapons. Wherever possible the tanks deployed into combat formation, raking the barrier with artillery fire. Most often, because narrow roads forced the tanks to stay in line, only the first tank was able to use its artillery. Of course, there was no one at or even near the barrier. Terrain features and antitank mines made it difficult for the tanks to circumnavigate the barrier. Sometimes the Soviets called supporting artillery to destroy the barrier, occasionally their engineers or infantry scouted fords to bypass destroyed bridges — a time-consuming process. That was the whole idea: to slow down the advance, to buy time, to delay and stop the enemy.

To remain under cover until the tank came into killing range required the greatest discipline. The advertised effective range of the Panzerfaust was 80 meters, but Corporal Schwertfeger told us to wait until the tank got within 30 or 40 meters of our position. According to him, "You can't hit shit beyond this range." Although a reliable tank killer, in addition to its short effective range the Panzerfaust had another distinct disadvantage: It signaled the launcher's location with a six-meter-long streak of fire and an unbelievably large, white plume of smoke and dust. Seconds after launch, every Soviet gun within view fired on the launcher's position; thus the escape trench into low cover. At a range of 30 meters you had but one chance for survival — you had to destroy that tank. You launched your antitank round. The tank killer team left the position immediately after firing the Panzerfaust. Others saw the graceful fiery tail as the rocket arched toward the rifleman's mortal enemy. The warhead impacted and penetrated the heavy armor plate. Molten steel spewed into the tank compartment; it set off secondary explosions. The frightening monster became an iron coffin because the hallelujah weapon had done its job. This tactic often created considerable confusion at the Soviet side. They had no idea how many undiscovered launchers were still there. Most often there were two or three still in hiding, but sometimes there were none.

As the terrain became ever more mountainous, as the roads became narrower, the Soviets realized that their tanks were no match for our mountains. Their attack stopped. During the resulting confusion we counterattacked. Actually the element that had attacked toward the rear was turned around and advanced through our line into the counterattack. Then — no one could say why — the Soviets just gave way and retreated to their original position across the Neisse River, and we swiftly followed them into our old position behind the cemetery and farm walls of Poischwitz.

On 19 April 1945 we heard that the High Command had ordered that all sixteen-year-olds were to be called up into the Wehrmacht while fourteen-year-olds and elderly men were mobilized in the *Volkssturm*. The lads at the Silesian Front had a good laugh; our local command at Bolkenhain was way ahead of the big wheels at German High Command in Berlin. Here every able male was already part of the armed forces either as a combatant or in engineering support groups building tank barriers or reinforcing strong points and small bunkers along the road.

Further orders from the Führer's headquarters were announced, but no one paid much attention to these ridiculous pronouncements. They seemed to come from somewhere totally divorced from our Sudeten Mountains region — or from reality.

Chapter 16

The Russian Boy

During one of our nightly forays into the Soviet line, I and one of the veterans became separated from our patrol. Unexpectedly we found Soviets teeming in the street and the surrounding gardens. We took cover in the basement of a row house while the rest of our patrol withdrew. For a moment we were safe. However, as we cowered in the basement we heard several dull explosions; the Soviets were systematically clearing buildings by throwing hand grenades into each basement, a standard street fighting practice. Desperately we searched for a way out. In the almost total darkness I thought I saw the outline of a break in the basement wall. I remembered that in the early 1940s all basement walls of row houses had been pierced with door-like openings, escape tunnels should one of the houses be destroyed in an air raid. I grabbed my partner and motioned him to follow. We raced from one basement into the next; explosions followed. Suddenly the sickeningly sweet stench of death hit my nostrils. Too late I had already stepped into a decaying corpse. I gagged, "What the hell was that?"

Gasping, the soldier behind me shouted, "Don't worry, his troubles are over. Keep going!"

Finally we reached the last house. Cold fresh air waved from its dark opening. As I emerged from the hole in the basement wall I saw a dark outline — actually the back of a small figure — fur cap, padded uniform, and the familiar PPSh with its large ammunition drum against the dark winter sky. A Soviet blocked our escape. Startled by our noisy exit he turned. For a split second I saw a young face, breath steaming into the bitter cold air. Instinctively he lifted his PPSh.

All motion, all time, the whole world, stopped. My machine pistol fired. The first two or three rounds smashed uselessly into the snow, but the recoil of explosions pulled the muzzle of my gun upward and to the right. Five, six, seven 9-mm copper-coated, lead parabellum rounds slammed into the back and side of the boy's heavy quilted uniform like a swarm of angry hornets. Powdery puffs of dusty snow rose from his shoulders. The impact of the bullets pulled the young Russian upward. The fur cap flew from his head, the PPSh from his hands. He dropped, face first, into the snow. His body jerked ever so slightly — then lay still. I stood frozen, desperate, frightened, my fingers still cramped around the trigger of the now silent and empty machine pistol. For a moment it was agonizingly quiet. Then the older soldier, still running for his life, crashed into me. We both fell into the snow. Gasping for air I raised up and looked around. Only inches away lay the silent figure crumpled in the snow, his blue eyes wide open, staring, but no longer seeing, steam rising from the stubble of his closely cropped blond hair.

The soldier behind me whispered hoarsely, "They'll be here in no time." He hastily dragged me through the town's last gardens and, still in panic, we threw our combined weight against a lattice fence that broke with a dry crack. Like two frightened shadows we rushed into the open field; wildly unaimed automatic fire rattled behind us. Moments later a flare rose high above us. Its brilliant, stark, white light illuminated the village. We were outlined in its flickering light as we rushed across the open field toward the creek bed we had used — it seemed eons ago — to enter the village. More shots rang out, some from a machine gun. Tracer rounds arched in our general direction. Some fifty feet beyond the fence we plunged into a depression. Too late did we remember that there was waist-deep snow that now threatened to impede our flight. On hands and knees we clawed our way back to the edge of the ravine. Then, keeping just below the crest, we raced recklessly toward the German line.

Small arms fire, exploding grenades, and the flares that illuminated the dark winter sky had brought Combat Sector Poischwitz to high alert. The soldier and I were the last of the patrol to return. I was barely able to keep abreast of my comrade. It seemed we were too far to the left of the mine gate.

I pulled on his sleeve to stop him. I told him that I thought we were in the minefield. He looked around. And agreed with a curse. Then he paused for a moment and said that we must carefully get into a prone position, then crawl as flat as we could across the snow. He was sure this would lessen the pressure and, he thought, the ground was sufficiently frozen for us to slide across without setting off one of our own mines.

Carefully, very carefully, we placed first one knee, then the other, then one hand, then the other, onto the icy crust of the snow until we lay prone. Then we crawled ever so slowly across the minefield. The next 100 meters were pure torture; never knowing whether my comrade was right, but we had no choice but to advance. Near the outpost line the soldier motioned me to stop. Exhausted my head dropped into the snow; steam rose from my hot cheeks. "Now that we made it this far, it would be a shame to get shot by our own," the soldier whispered. He looked up. "Hey, Walter," he called into the darkness. "It's me, Heinrich."

Finally I had learned the name of my partner.

Heinrich pushed open the door of the warm farm kitchen, our bunker. He brushed aside the large blanket that served as a blackout curtain and shouted, "Hey guys, the boy got his first Ivan!" Several of the older men looked away. No one said anything. One turned to toss two more pieces of wood into the lively fire that had already turned the kitchen stove a glowing red. I stuttered that I had not meant to shoot him. Corporal Schwertfeger interrupted me saying that he was glad that the two of us were alive. The guys in the sector had heard the shooting. He pointed toward the rear where three men in winter gear were just returning equipment to the weapons rack and said that those three were coming to get us, and he thanked the Lord that it was not necessary. Only then did he notice the stench emanating from my boots. He paused, then asked whether I had shit in my pants when I shot that Ivan, or worse, whether I had died out there. Only then did I again notice the stench of decayed flesh. Now, in the warm kitchen, it smelled worse. He told me to get out of his abode, because he kept a nice place. Then, lowering his voice, he laughingly advised me to go to the shed, get some kerosene, brush my boots and whatever else stinks, and not to come back until the godawful smell was gone!

Although I had my trousers airing out all night in the harsh winter air, for days thereafter there still lingered the faint smell of kerosene. Here, in the front line, we used kerosene to light our lamps and to kill lice and fleas; an every-day nuisance.

We were once again at the Bolkenhain training and rest camp when we heard about terrible atrocities committed by the Soviets at Striegau, a neighboring town. In several counterattacks our forces had severely damaged the enemy, liberated the city of Lauban, and made the rail line into Upper Silesia once again operational. And, we heard that the 208th Division had liberated Striegau where the horrors committed against civilians by the Soviets had embittered the German soldier.[1] Two boys recovering from wounds told us that the low-life Soviet *pekhota*[2] had raped and murdered young girls and women, including eighty-year-old grandmothers. The *pekhota* had in the most bestial ways shot the men folk and then raped the women next to their husbands' and fathers' corpses. The boys told us that everyone was totally blown out of his mind seeing these atrocities. The boys said, however, that no matter what terrible crimes the *pekhota* had committed, they fought like cornered rats, and that the boys killed them all — like rats. As German troops retreated under strong Soviet counterattacks, the few Germans who survived the carnage hidden in attics and basements fled through Soviet and German small arms fire not caring whether they lived or died. They ran in terror. The boys said that the survivors were insane with fear and revulsion.[3]

After the incident with the Russian boy I had trouble sleeping. In my dreams I saw the young Russian's profile under the fur cap. I saw as he turned, as my bullets slammed into his young body, and then I saw the huddled figure in the snow. My uniform was clean again, my boots no longer smelled of death — but would I ever forget the startled look on the face of that Russian boy as his life ebbed away in the snow?

With every day our military situation worsened. The 1st Ukrainian Front had now reached Görlitz, far to our west, and on 24 March 1945, the 4th Ukrainian Front captured Sorau, having broken through the German LIX Korps on a front of ten miles to a depth of five miles. Five German divisions were surrounded southwest of Oppeln.[4] With the 4th Ukrainian Front advancing through the Mährisch-Ostrau gap into our rear we stood in danger of being cut off from the rest of the Reich — or whatever was left of it. All of Silesia, with the exception of the narrow sliver along the Sudeten Mountains, was in enemy hands. Could matters really get any worse? We were now sandwiched between the 1st and the 4th Ukrainian fronts and, should elements of the 1st Ukrainian Front break southward from Görlitz through the Elbe River gap, we would be entirely cut off from the Reich.

During the hours of darkness activity along the road between Poischwitz and Bolkenhain continued at a brisk pace. We, along with Corporal Schwertfeger and the other soldiers, were relieved by fresh troops. We walked a few miles into the mountains, and there, hidden under the

> Das Lebensgut dankst
> du würdigen Ahnen.
> Dir weiset dein Wünschen
> und Wille den Weg. Der
> Wirkende bist du, der
> Bürge der Zukunft, dein
> ist der Tag.
>
> Treu der Scholle
> Treu dem Volk
> Treu der Sippe
> Und getreu dir selbst!
>
> Lerne Leiden ohne zu
> klagen!
>
> Bilder um Bilder um=
> flogen sie; Vater in seiner
> grünen Lodenjoppe —
> frohes Ballspiel mit
> den Schwestern hinter

Above: Quotations. *Opposite:* A sketch of one of the much feared Soviet *pekhota. Author's diary.*

Chapter 16 — The Russian Boy

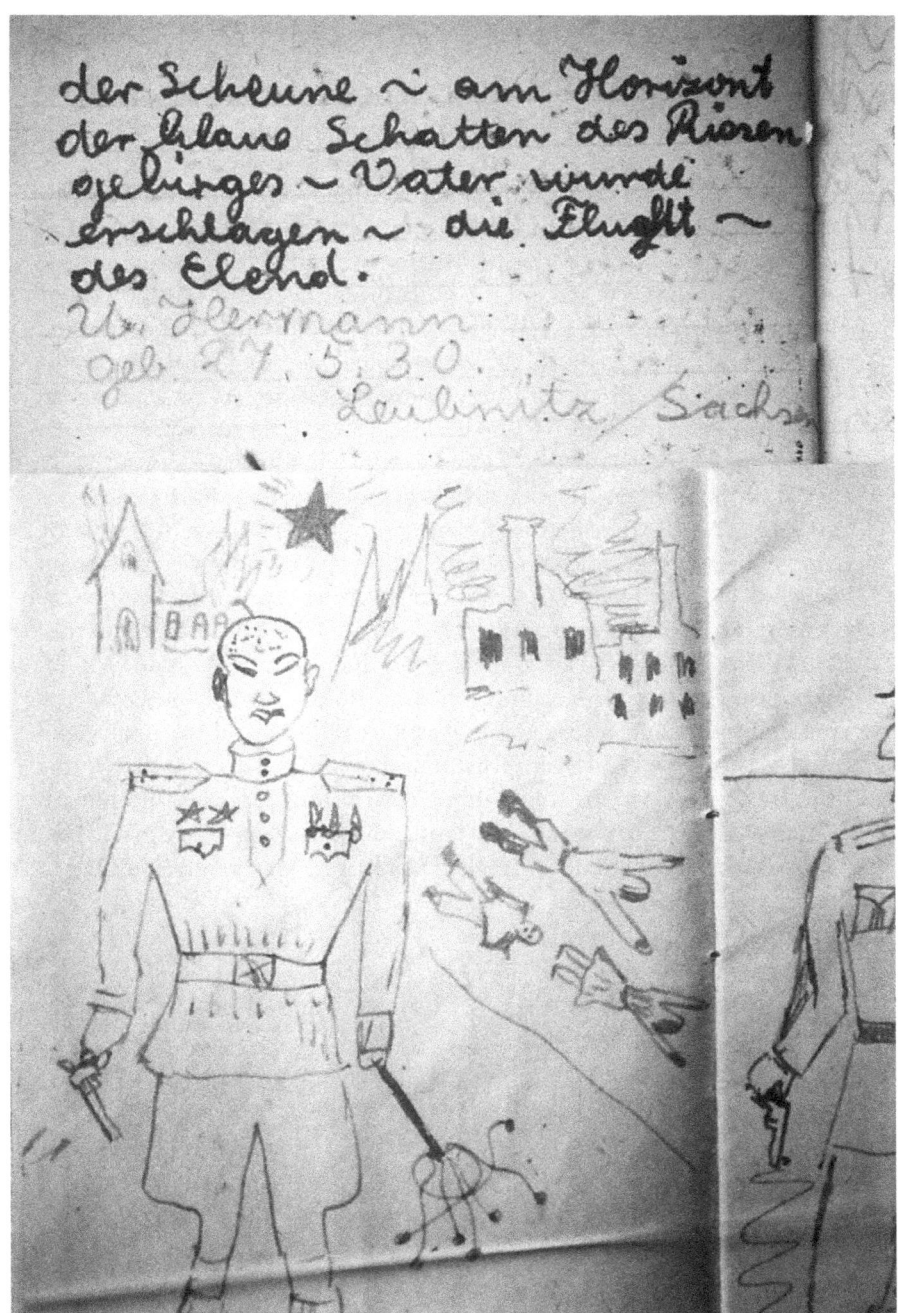

thick canopy of fir trees, mounted trucks for the short ride to the rear. Once again at our base camp near the Bolko castle we turned in our filthy uniforms for delousing and cleaned our bodies of the grime of frontline life. Hot chow and fresh clothing soon restored the morale of the soldiers. But, only a week or so later we were back on the line.

After long hours of standing guard, bunker and gun position maintenance, and training, the simple German Army chow of stew, bread, and coffee or tea was our best reward. During the chill of the evenings those not on guard duty sat around the potbellied stoves and hungrily shoveled pea soup, heavily laden with potatoes, a few pieces of smoked sausage, and whatever Little Erich was able to scrounge from the abandoned nearby dwellings into hungry mouths. The last bits were then wiped from the mess gear with slices of hearty rye bread. Then we sat on our bunks and listened to Little Erich playing his harmonica.

And, once again, we came back to our favorite training camp for rest and recuperation, that is, the usual hot water shower followed by delousing and the issuance of clean uniforms. By now we considered ourselves seasoned veterans. Even our sergeant cast a more kindly eye on us and, as you may remember, he had only one. But Sergeant One-Eye drilled the new arrivals to the limit of their capacities — and beyond.

I still had trouble sleeping. I had not told anyone of my reoccurring nightmare and of the young Russian's white profile as it smashed into the snow. Would I ever forget it and dream the dreams that young boys are supposed to dream? of girls? The training sergeants did not tell us about that part of the war, of death and destruction. They just joked, "These boys are General Schörner's last resort." Most likely, they had to contend with their own nightmares.

Chapter 17

"Routine" Patrol

It was supposed to be just another routine patrol before midnight in late March. We entered a cleared path in one of our minefields. Our point man had already cleared the mine gap and taken up a defensive position some 50 or 60 feet away. Suddenly the stillness of the night was shattered by a bright flash and a dull crack. The man just in front of me had stepped on a *Schuhmine* small antipersonnel mine — explosives in a small wooden box with one trip fuse. I, just a few paces behind the unfortunate one, had instantaneously closed my eyes. I was knocked to the ground. My right leg felt as if a hard brushwood broom had whipped across it. Corporal Schwertfeger, leading the patrol, whispered — God knows why, everyone within miles must have heard the explosion — for no one to move. "There are mines all around us," he said urgently. "Those Russian bastards must have planted a few shoe mines in our 'mine-free' alley."

He crawled toward us carefully probing the ground with his bayonet. He looked at the bloody leg of the man who had stepped on the mine. He cut the soldier's trousers with a pocket knife. I had landed with my head just inches from the other man's boot. I saw the man's foot just dangling by a thin strip of skin. The corporal quickly severed the last part of the man's skin. The foot, still in the shredded boot, fell to the ground. A tourniquet, expertly applied, stopped the bleeding. Meanwhile the corpsman, the last man in the patrol, hastily crawled over us so as not to step on a mine. He and Corporal Schwertfeger bandaged the stump. The wounded man started to breathe heavily and moaned; from the medical kit the corpsman took a syringe and injected a shot of morphine. Corporal Schwertfeger again whispered for everyone to keep quiet, and was anyone else hurt? Since my knee had started to ache I looked and saw blood all over my right trouser leg. I grabbed his arm and pointed at my leg. Before I realized it, the pocket knife was back in his hand and he cut away my right trouser leg. For a split second I thought he was also going to cut off my leg, but he just stripped off the trouser leg so the corpsman could bandage my knee. Then he passed word to the point man that we would retrace our route and return to our lines. There was no sense going any farther, the enemy all knew where we were.

The wounded soldier and I were brought to the field aid station. After a quick check our corpsman pinned "wounded" tags on our tunics; then they loaded us into an ambulance. It was more than an hour's ride to the field hospital at Landeshut. My unfortunate comrade disappeared into the operating room while I waited. Well after midnight a doctor looked at my leg and opined that my leg did not look as bad as my buddy's. He would have that fixed in no time. The hospital was short on anesthetics. The doctor thought nothing of using a pair of tweezers to pick bits of dirt, wood, and metal out of my leg without any type of pain killer. There must have been hundreds of pieces. An eternity later he washed my leg with iodine, which almost made me shoot through the ceiling, put on a light bandage, and placed me on one of the hospital cots to sleep.

My wounds were just shallow scratches from particles that had managed to penetrate my three layers of clothing — long woolen underwear, heavy gray woolen trousers, and white camouflage coveralls. I took a hot bath with my right leg out of the tub so as not to wet the bandages. It was the first time in months that I was almost totally submerged in hot water; what a great feeling. The next morning I received a totally new set of uniforms. It seemed as if I had grown somewhat. The uniform was no longer two sizes too large and uncomfortable; now it actually seemed to fit quite well. Around noon I found my fellow patrol member. To my utter surprise, he was in high spirits. He gleefully told me that this was the best thing that had ever happened to him, a *Heimatschuss*.[1] He would leave for home in a day or two.

I was startled. How could anyone be happy about losing a foot? Undeterred he continued to tell me that this war had turned to shit. That for him it was the only way out of there, and if the whole thing blew up, as it would, he advised me to not stop along the way. He told me to be sure to make it to Bavaria. He wrote down his address and told me to come and his mother would have a bed for me. No problem. He handed me a slip of paper on which was written his mother's address in

The author with his sister, Helga, in Czechoslovakia during a short convalescent leave. *Author's collection.*

fine print. I had not known his name until that moment. He was Sebastian Trenker and came from a small village south of München.

That afternoon the duty sergeant told me to pack my satchel and leave for home in the morning and wait there until my puncture wounds had healed. I wanted to say my farewell to Sebastian the next morning, but I was told he was already on a train for a military hospital at Munich. His wish had come true — he had gotten his *Heimatschuss*.

With my two-way army transportation chit in my pocket and my haversack filled with bread, sausages, six or seven pieces of chocolate from emergency rations, and a half pound of good coffee — not the common *Ersatzkaffee*—I headed for the train station. The 10 o'clock train for Trautenau left exactly on time. There I changed to the local "milk train" and arrived at Altenbuchen in the early afternoon. For my family and friends it was a great surprise. I had not had time to write of my misadventure. My mother and Preuss Oma thought I "had grown a whole head taller" during the past few months. All the children wanted to see my injured leg. Sweet Susi came by to console me. We made several attempts to get away from all the children — my cousins and neighbors — by walking toward the nearby woods to "exercise my wounded leg." Every attempt ended in failure. Every kid in the neighborhood tagged along. So much for being a "hero." Since my wounds were mostly shallow lacerations, they healed rather quickly. In less than two weeks, over Mother's strenuous objections, I was ready to return to the front.

Chapter 18

Ah, Natascha

After a long farewell and a comfortable train ride from Altenbuchen I arrived at Landeshut rail station in the early afternoon. The local transportation sergeant at the train station gave me another transportation chit and told me to report to the training camp of *Kampfkommandant* Bolkenhain for further assignment. The train to Bolkenhain was already waiting on the track, the engine hooked up and steaming. The passenger compartments exuded a cozy warmth. The train would not leave until dusk, because the last stretch of track was under observation by the Soviets who lobbed artillery shells on anything that moved. I had a bit to eat at the army canteen, walked a little around the waiting rooms, looked at some of the numerous propaganda posters — just to kill time. When I finally climbed aboard the train, it seemed I was one of the first arrivals. The passenger cars were almost empty. I entered a compartment, shut the door, stretched out on the wooden bench, and rolled myself into my blanket. It was cozy, warm, and secure and I fell asleep almost immediately. Periodically I heard steam pipes crackling in the heating system, doors opening and closing, heavy steps fading in the passageway — all the ambient noises of a rail car in waiting.

The scraping of the sliding door of my compartment awakened me. A timid female voice asked, "Is this compartment reserved?" Drowsily I looked up. There stood a young woman — a girl, really — with an infant in one arm and a large clothing bag draped over the other. I untangled myself from my blanket. "No, no. I am the only one here." I cleared my knapsack from the other bench. She slid through the door and closed it again. The baby was still asleep. The girl dropped the bag on the floor. I jumped up and lifted it onto the bench as she placed a blanket and small pillow next to the bag and settled the baby into a cocoon-like nest. I introduced myself. She said, "I am Natascha," and waited. I did not know what to say.

"My mother loved reading pre–World War One Russian books. She fell in love with the name Natascha. That's why I am called Natascha."

"Oh," I managed to say, "that's a lovely name, unusual for a German girl to be called Natascha, but beautiful."

We started to talk about names, where we came from, where we were going. She told me the baby's name was Helga, and I told her about my sister, Helga. "At least your child does not have to give an explanation every time she introduces herself."

We both laughed at that. She told me that the baby's father had disappeared. "We were supposed to have gotten married the day after New Year's, but he could not get leave from the Eastern Front. He is missing in action." She looked terribly sad as if this were the first time she had ever consciously spoken of her daughter's father, now most likely no longer among the living. "His last letter arrived before Christmas."

In January she had received a notice from the army that he was missing in action. She had fled on a roundabout way from Sorau to Bolkenhain, and was on her way back to Bolkenhain from the Landeshut hospital where her baby had been examined and had received inoculations. We talked about her home town. I mentioned that from the front line I could see Jauer, my home town, that I had been at the edge of that town several times during night patrols, but never near my Grandfather's farm.

We were so engrossed in our reminiscing we did not realize that dusk had approached. Each compartment was illuminated by one small, blue, blackout lamp. We heard the conductor announcing, "All aboard," and moments later, with steam hissing, clouds of white water vapor rising, the train started to move, at first hesitantly. Landeshut rapidly disappeared from view. The train entered the first of many serpentine curves steaming through the dark pine forest. Along the way the baby started to indicate it was uncomfortable. The girl — now totally a mother — changed the baby's diaper, then held her so it could look through the window at the pine trees rushing past. However, the baby was still uncomfortable; her mother knew it was past feeding time. She looked at me somewhat self-consciously and said, "I hope you don't mind," as she positioned her baby and gently exposed one of her breasts. The baby eagerly sought the nipple for nourishment. I observed every

Chapter 18 — Ah, Natascha

detail: a beautiful, pale breast, a dark nipple, and a happy baby, all in the wonderful dimness of the passenger compartment. I became embarrassed when I looked up and saw Natascha watching me. I must have turned purple, although darkness kindly hid it from Natascha.

"Have you never seen a baby nursed?" she asked.

"Not for many years," I managed to stutter.

"Don't be embarrassed! It's the most wonderful thing on earth. It's also very practical. Just think: no bottles, no milk to buy. I carry it all in me." I thought about it, and I wanted to say that the container looked pretty good to me too.

"Actually," Natascha said, "you are the first man to ever see Helga being nursed. Not even her father has seen it." She paused, then continued sadly, "Of course, he has never seen the baby."

I did not know what to say; neither did Natascha. The train rolled slowly toward Bolkenhain. I wanted it to slow down even more. I really enjoyed being with Natascha and her baby. After a while, at first hesitatingly, we continued our conversation. She told me how she had ended up in Bolkenhain. There she had quarters in a row house owned by a brash old lady. Natascha had one room, a comfortable one with a cooking stove and water faucet and laundry sink. It was just what she needed to take care of her baby. When I told her that I was going to the training camp atop the hill across the town from the castle, she said, "But we arrive after midnight. That's a long walk in the cold of the night. Is someone expecting you?"

"No one knows I am coming." I told her about the problem with my leg, my recovery at Altenbuchen, and why I left to come back to the front. She laughed about my misadventure with Susi and "walking to strengthen the leg."

"Did you really think you could fool those kids?" she asked.

"Of course. No one knows what we did last year," I replied.

Natascha just laughed. "You are so innocent. I just love that." Again I turned purple.

The baby had fallen asleep. Natascha discreetly moved the baby's head and tucked her breast into her bodice — not so discreetly that I could not get a long look at the most beautiful breast I had ever seen. Even more beautiful than Susi's. Natascha tucked her baby under the blankets on the bench, then moved over to sit next to me. We talked again about life and death as we knew it, about love, the world, heaven and earth, until she said, "Now, tell me, are you going to walk all the way through town and up that hill in the middle of the night, or are you coming with me? I live only two blocks from the station."

Somewhat startled I said, "How can I refuse that offer?"

She replied, "Good, then, it's all settled."

We sat in silence for a long time, both probably contemplating the agreement. The train rolled through the thick pine forests until suddenly the trees were no longer there. I turned to Natascha. "Come to the window and look. Soon we will turn the last curve on this mountain. Then you can see our whole beautiful Silesian lowlands. Far in the distance you can see the front line. There are always some lights, flares, fires, some tracers curving into the sky. But, this is what it's all about."

As the train turned into the last curve — "See, look, what a beautiful sight it is!" — We both craned our necks, standing close to each other, observing what few of our kind would ever see again — our Silesian homeland.

> Blue mountains
> Green valleys
> Among all, a small cottage
> This land
> is Silesia, my home.[1]

The train eased its way down the mountain and into the station. As it creaked to a halt the station master was there to signal us in. Also there and ready was the crew from army supply that would rapidly unload ammunition, food, and other gear; the train had to leave a good hour before sunup or come under long-range Soviet artillery fire. Natascha bundled her baby into blankets to shield her from the crisp winter air. I grabbed my and Natascha's bags and we left the station together — like a soldier and his wife returning.

We walked through crunching snow the few city blocks to a row house. Natascha pulled out a large key from somewhere and opened the front door. We walked into a darkened entranceway and closed the door — blackout. Natascha felt the wall for the light switch and a very dim bulb glimmered at the far end of the hall. She walked briskly to one of the first floor apartment doors, extracted another key, and opened her little sanctuary. She, the baby, and I with the two bags entered as quietly as we could. Natascha closed the door, turned on the light, and placed the baby in her makeshift crib. I dropped the bags on the floor and surveyed Natascha's home. It looked comfortable, small but neat.

Helga slept the sleep of the innocent. Natascha busied herself with the stove. I moved over to help — I always was a good fire maker. Soon a small fire crackled in the stove. Its flickering flames added a certain charm to the surroundings. I saw Natascha standing somewhat sadly, as she discreetly placed a framed photograph into the drawer near the baby's crib. Then she turned around to look at me. "Let's heat lots of water. First we'll make some tea, then we'll fill the *Sitzbad*.[2] After all our travels we both could probably use a hot bath."

I mumbled some sort of agreement. We filled one small teakettle and two enormous pots with water from the faucet. I could already see how convenient this little apartment was. As the room became warmer I removed my greatcoat and tunic, then sat down to feed the fire while Natascha busied herself around the room. She checked on Helga, and took off her quilted coat, scarf, and golden-brown woolen jacket. Now she looked less like a mother and much more like a young girl. She was not even eighteen years old, dark blonde hair tied in an old-fashioned bun, not quite as tall as I, not heavy, but with a well-developed figure. She flew around the room fixing this, setting up that, opening the cupboard to get tea, wiping tea glasses, spoons, until she ran out of things to do. She stopped, looked at me, and laughed. "Look at me, acting like a silly young girl."

I looked. "Certainly not silly." We both laughed.

"We can't make too much noise, the old landlady even complains that the baby's crying disturbs her sleep."

With that we sat together on her bed and watched the fire, flames flickering along the wall. She briefly touched my hand. The water in the small teakettle had started to hum. When steam rose from the kettle she flew to prepare the tea the old-fashioned way — four teaspoons of loose tea in a four-cup pot. To the makeshift table near the stove she brought brown wartime sugar, two spoons per glass, and filled the glasses to the rim with the steaming brew. For a long time we sat sipping the sweet, hot tea, watching the flickering fire, and looking at each other, not saying a word.

After a long silence I asked her if she would object if I told her what had been on my mind for a long time — besides her beautiful body, of course. She laughed and said, "Say your piece."

I gathered my thoughts. I told her about reports that Soviet troops, ordered by Stalin and encouraged by persons like the noted Soviet poet Ehrenburg to "kill, kill, and to spare no one," had followed those orders only too well. I told her that this was not just some of Herr Goebbels' propaganda. Then I told her about one of our counterattacks where we had liberated a small section of a village that had been occupied by Soviet infantry for only a short time. I told her about Striegau, where Soviet troops raped, plundered, burned, and killed civilians and soldiers indiscriminantly, that we found old farmers, women, and children murdered in the most horrible ways. I told her that the Soviets fought like cornered rats. I told her that after seeing all this we had taken no prisoners, that we had killed the entire bunch of savages. I told her it had been easier than shooting dogs. I told her of all the horrors I had witnessed, had suppressed, and had never dared to let surface, not even in my innermost thoughts. Looking into her eyes, thinking of her baby, it suddenly all poured out of me. I then took her hand in mine and pleaded with her to leave Bolkenhain; I begged her to leave this comfortable little place that she had created on tomorrow night's train and to never come back here. I told her about Sebastian, the fellow who was wounded with me. I pulled his address from my tunic and asked her to go to Bavaria, to tell Sebastian's mother about him and about me, and to tell her that I asked that she give Natascha quarters, and that I would try to get to Munich if at all possible. I pulled the slightly soiled and folded note Sebastian Trenker had written before he left on the ambulance train to München, his home district, from my breast pocket and placed it into her hand. She looked at me for a long time, tears streaming over her cheeks, and then she kissed the tears on my face. Only then did I realize I too was crying.

We sat together until the steam rose from these two large pots on the stove. Together we emptied the first pot into the *Sitzbad*; Natascha tested the water — too hot — and slowly added cold water from a pail until she thought the bathwater was just right. "You go first," she urged me. "You might need it more than I." I laughed. The laughter woke the baby, who grunted. It was feeding time again. Amazing how this lovely young girl transformed herself almost instantaneously into a caring mother. She picked up the baby, cuddled her against her chest, freed one of her breasts from her blouse — she had no brassiere — and guided the baby to the dark brown nipple. Baby made eager suckling noises. This time I watched it all with utter amazement. Natascha was right, it was indeed the most wonderful thing on earth, and practical to boot — as well as very arousing.

Soon the baby was fed and she fell asleep immediately. Natascha wrapped Helga in her swaddling cloth and, in an instant, became a young girl again. With my arousal I was just a little embarrassed, but Natascha helped me out of the rest of my uniform, stripped off the scratchy field-gray woolen underwear, and gently pushed me into the cozy, warm water of the *Sitzbad*. Only then did she notice the black and blue scars on my right knee. She was horrified. "I thought you told me the wounds had all healed?" Her nurturing instinct took over. With the warm, soft washcloth she carefully soaped my wounded leg. Looking at my arousal her impishness returned. "I see none of the most important vital parts are damaged." With the warm water all tension drained from my body and soul as I relaxed in the semidarkness of Natascha's sanctuary. Natascha poured water over my hair, handed me a piece of good laundry soap to scrub my hair and body, then helped with the rinsing. I stepped out of the tub newly born. Natascha threw a towel at me while she slid out of her blouse and skirt. She wore heavy woolen underwear and long woolen stockings. Momentarily her alabaster white body gleamed in the flickering flames of the stove as she, totally uninhibited, slipped gently into the water. With the washcloth I scrubbed her back, her neck, and, very tenderly, her breasts. She leaned back her head and slowly closed her chestnut-brown eyes as I leaned over to kiss her forehead.

From the bed I watched as Natascha dried herself and, still covered by the bath towel, walked to check her baby. She turned and let the towel slowly slip to the floor, then joined me under the thick, fluffy featherbed. We explored each other's bodies, then became one.

I was in paradise.

Late in the night we fell asleep in each other's arms. Once or twice during the early morning hours I vaguely became aware of murmurs and suckling noises; Natascha was nursing her baby. The aroma of strong tea awoke me. Natascha, already fully dressed, had busied herself making fire, taking care of the baby's needs, and preparing tea. I jumped from bed and quickly dressed so that I could help empty the bath water. Once again I watched as Natascha miraculously switched between young girl and mother almost instantaneously. She poured her aromatic brew into two large glasses, cut several slices of black *Bauernbrot*,[3] covered them with the usual wartime marmalade. My first experience having breakfast with a wonderful woman.

"My landlady has left to do her morning shopping. She won't be back for at least half an hour." I took this to mean that Natascha did not wish to be compromised by my presence. After I had finished my bread and tea I first kissed the baby, then held Natascha far longer than I had ever held a girl.

"Promise me that you will leave!" She solemnly nodded her lovely head. "Promise me that you will seek refuge in Bavaria, that you will talk to Sebastian's mother. Tell her about us. Who knows what will happen, but if all goes well, I will see you there. Whatever happens then, we'll see. Good luck."

She held my hand for just another second, then looked into the hallway. The coast was clear. I left the house hurriedly, walked through town and up the hill toward the camp without ever looking back. I dared not. I would not have been able to withstand the pain.

Chapter 19

To the Bitter End

I had left Natascha's place reluctantly and walked through town and up the hill to the replacement camp. Sergeant One-Eye told me to stay at the training camp until my leg was completely healed. He treated me almost like a real soldier.

In early April 1945 the radio announced that the Russians were continuing the systematic liquidation of the encircled German garrison at Breslau, which was holding out gallantly. General Schörner, our commander of Army Group Center, defending Czechoslovakia, became a field marshal. It was news to us that he had available to him the most numerous and efficient branch of the Wehrmacht, with about 1.2 million men. The commentator admitted that the forces opposing him were superior in number, armament, and morale.[1]

A few days later Corporal Schwertfeger and his group, with Lothar and some of the other boys from Poischwitz, returned to the camp. Little Erich was not among them. Lothar said that Little Erich had gotten killed in one those stupid little skirmishes that escaped all but the most minute mentioning in dispatches. They had buried Little Erich with full military honors at the cemetery where he had died. The old veterans had fired three scattered volleys. Everyone was in deep sorrow. Later Lothar whispered that Corporal Schwertfeger had been almost insane when he found that Little Erich had been killed — he had promised to protect him from harm and had failed.

All the new boys undergoing training under the tutelage of Sergeant One-Eye had to pull guard duty, police the area, sweep the wooden sidewalks, and do other sundry housekeeping tasks. We, the old-timers, were here almost on vacation. Toward us, Sergeant One-Eye was almost benevolent. The new trainees viewed us with added respect when Sergeant One-Eye told them about some of the exploits of "his boys," we, the ones he had castigated just two months ago. He told them how his boys, who had barely become acquainted with the *Panzerfaust*, had destroyed several T-34 tanks, and how we had, although encircled during a Soviet counterattack, defended our position for several hours until relieved by a counterattack. We tried not to show our pride, but we relished the newly found admiration from those who had not yet been at the front.

On the 20th of April 1945 came the announcement that the Führer celebrated his 56th birthday in his Berlin bunker, while battles raged from the Sudeten Mountains to the Gulf of Stettin. This time no store windows were decorated, no parades celebrated the event. Instead, at night we held guessing games: Which of the sergeant's eyes is the glass eye? The next day we tried to see who made the right guess. It was difficult, because when the sergeant stared his men down, they forgot which eye swiveled and which did not.

Sergeant One-Eye gave the old-timers Sunday off. I guess, now that he had turned us into the "most efficient killing machine the world has ever known," he thought we deserved a break. Lothar, I, and a few others went into downtown Bolkenhain that morning. I walked past Natascha's place several times before I got up enough courage to knock on the door. The old lady, the owner of the house, came out. I asked whether I could talk to Natascha. The old lady, a real mean old bitch, began to shout, "That young one? I'll tell you where she went. She left, told me about what the Russians will do to us women when they get here. She heard it from one of the soldiers. It wasn't you, was it?" She gestured at me with her scrawny, crooked finger. All I could think of was the old witch in Grimms' fairy tale *Hansel und Gretel*. "I told her that the soldier who told her those lies should be shot for *Wehrkraftzersetzung*.[2] It wasn't you, was it? It wasn't you?" she repeated and again pointed her crooked finger at me. "I told her to stay here and trust our boys in uniform. They'll keep those Russians where they belong, I told her. Soon there will come the counterattack the Führer has promised, and those Russians will be back in Russia, where they belong, I told her. But, no, she believed what that rotten excuse of a soldier told her. He should be shot, I told her!" We walked, then ran away, with her cackling voice fading in the distance. "The Führer promised. He always keeps his word, you'll see...."

That woman was dangerous. We ran to get away from that cantankerous bitch. Around the next street corner, and after we had caught our collective breaths, Lothar asked, "What the hell that was all about? Who the hell is Natascha? She wasn't talking about you, was she?" He thought that old bag was dangerous, that she could get us all into deep trouble. I told the guys that I had met Natascha on the train, we had talked, and I had told her about Striegau, and that I was the one who had begged Natascha to leave. They all talked at once to tell me that I was totally insane, that the old bitch could get us all killed. Then they asked, how could I have been so stupid? I had no answer to the last question. With all the talk about the penalty for "undermining the fighting spirit of the German Armed Forces" they forgot to query me about my relationship with Natascha — and I was glad. I never could have told them about the wonders of life — and they never would have believed me anyway. On the way back to camp one of the others thought that the old bitch would never have to worry about some Russian grabbing her. She would be too tough even for them.

Once in a while there was some good news. One evening the radio announcer proclaimed that new forces were rushing to Berlin.

> Achtung, achtung. Das Oberkommando
> der Wehrmacht gibt bekannt.
>
> 1 May 1945. At the center of the city of Berlin the brave defenders are gathered around our Führer in the heroic struggle against the Bolshevik masses.[3]

Goebbels reported that we had sufficient weapons to defend the nation's capital, and that any messages that we were capitulating were attempts by enemy propagandists to destroy our will to fight. We remembered Sergeant One-Eye's edict, "Bullshit. Nothing but bullshit from Berlin." Someone in the barracks said that Führer means "leader," so he was leading — big deal. Everyone laughed. Under the guidance of Sergeant One-Eye, our prime cynic, we had all become cynics — and it really felt good.

Lothar, I, and the other boys from our group remained at the training camp. Sergeant One-Eye kept us there to help in training the new boys on the block. Since the beginning of May the weather had become downright summery. We had passed directly from a cold and nasty winter into a beautiful late spring. The fruit orchards below our hill, the gardens, and the meadow were in full bloom, and life, aside from the war, became almost bearable. However, all the news was bad.

> Achtung, achtung. Das Oberkommando
> der Wehrmacht gibt bekannt.
>
> 2 May 1945. The Führer has died leading the heroic defenders of the nation's capital. He sacrificed his life steeped in the knowledge that his struggle would save his *Volk* and Europe from the destruction of Bolshevism.[4]

When we told Sergeant One-Eye that the Führer had died a hero's death in Berlin his only comment was, "What else but a hero's death?" Later we heard that Grand Admiral Dönitz, the commander in chief of the navy, would make an important announcement. The surprise announcement was that the Führer had named him his successor as head of state and supreme commander of all German forces. He had accepted command of those forces with the intention to continue the battle against Bolshevism until the fighting elements, and the hundreds of thousands of families in Germany's eastern territories, had been secured from enslavement or destruction. He would continue the fight against the British and Americans as long as they obstructed this fight against Bolshevism.

Someone at the training camp wondered, Whatever happened to our glorious Reichsmarschall? We did not know, but thought Göring was next in command. Someone said, "Obermaier?" The whole barracks broke out in hilarious laughter. I had not realized that my former classmate's political joke was so widely known that this single word could produce communal laughter. No one knew what had happened to Obermaier or where he was hiding — and no one cared.

It was strange, though, a navy man leading what was essentially a ground war. And, once again the battle against the Soviets raged farther north. General Krebs, German Army chief of staff, offered to negotiate the surrender of the Berlin garrison to the Soviets. The Soviets demanded unconditional surrender. General Krebs returned to the command bunker, informed the leadership, and then left to commit suicide. Shortly thereafter Goebbels killed his six children, then he and his wife committed suicide. Later we heard that the Soviets had captured Berlin on the 2nd of May and wondered, or maybe not, about previous reports that new forces were rushing to Berlin, and Goebbels' report that we had sufficient weapons to defend the nation's capital. As Sergeant One-Eye would say, "All, bullshit. Nothing but bullshit from Berlin."

Our state capital, surrounded since last January, had finally succumbed to the constant attacks by rear area Soviet forces. We wondered, now that the Soviets had captured Breslau. How long it would be before their whole might was deployed against us? There was not much more room to retreat. Soviet forces were advancing steadily into our rear through Czechoslovakia until only a narrow east-west corridor remained in German hands. We were sandwiched in. Bad news begets bad news. Now that Germany was breathing its last death rattles, the Czechs had started an uprising in Prague.

> Achtung, achtung. Das Oberkommando
> der Wehrmacht gibt bekannt.
> 6 May 1945. All is quiet along the Silesian Front and in Saxony.[5]

We remained in the barracks until the 7th or 8th of May. It was clear to all of us that the war had come to a bitter end. Intermittently, for almost three months, we had served as boy soldiers with the insane thoughts that we could save our homes. Now we received orders to retreat farther into the mountains. We loaded horse-drawn wagons with all the foodstuffs still in the kitchen. Early the next morning we fell in and marched out of camp. After a long, hard hike my unit reached Hirschberg. The next morning we were to cross the Sudeten Mountains via the Hirschberger Pass into Czechoslovakia. Our company was quartered in a high school gymnasium for the night. A mobile army kitchen unit served great tasting potato soup and the usual hot sausages, black bread, and butter to this bunch of always hungry teenagers. The following morning our company commander told us of another change in plans. Heavy snow blocked the Hirschberger Pass. He told us to gather our gear, fill our haversacks with food, take a basic load of ammo and our weapons, and strike out on our own. He cautioned us not to let anyone stop us. It was an order.

Only the Landeshuter Pass into Czechoslovakia, where our parents had found refuge, was open. Someone mentioned that the German railroad was still operating. Lothar and I decided we had walked just about far enough; now it was time to ride the train. With all the incongruity of war, the German railroad was indeed still operating, on schedule and on time.

So, on the 8th or 9th of May Lothar and I rode a train back toward the front line. The train arrived at Landeshut on schedule. Inside the terminal everything appeared to be normal. There was the usual buzz of activity: passengers hurried to catch trains or to meet friends or relatives, and the loudspeaker announced train departures, etc., totally normal for any railroad station. However, once we emerged from the semidarkness of the station into the brilliant sunshine of the plaza an unbelievable spectacle unfolded before us. Motor vehicles of all types, horse-drawn wagons loaded with soldiers and civilians, families with all their worldly goods on pushcarts or wheelbarrows, people with bicycles loaded to capacity, walkers with heavy knapsacks surged on both lanes of the road southward toward the only mountain pass not blocked by heavy snow.

Since we were armed Lothar and I quickly found seats as antiaircraft guards on the fenders of an army truck. Near Goldenau we left the crowded main escape road and hitched a ride on a wagon driven by a lone Russian SS volunteer. At long last we were on the way to Trautenau. There we climbed aboard another train: destination westward to Hohenelbe. Along the way some crazy Czech, probably thinking the train was loaded with civilians, fired a shot. He certainly received, if he lived to tell about it, the surprise of his life: rifle and machine pistol fire spit from every train window. Deadly lead saturated the hill, churned the whole side of the hill into a cloud of dust.

We were certain that our parents had long ago left Altenbuchen for sanctuary in Bavaria, and we planned to stay on the train. As the train passed the village we saw to our dismay the family's covered wagons — the *Trek* had never moved. We debarked quickly to join our families. Even before we reached their homes we disassembled our weapons and threw them in the nearby creek.

When Soviet elements broke southward through the Elbe River gap from Dresden, escape to the west was no longer possible. Our families were greatly relieved to see us. Our mothers made shorts out of our fieldgray army trousers. Mother removed all military emblems and the large uniform pockets. Then she washed the shorts and the tunics in a mixture concocted from black tea. They became an ugly dark brown, but at least the military field gray was gone. We retrieved our old shirts and once again became just boys.

Preoccupied by our concern for survival we missed one of the most important announcements from the German High Command — and its last message. On 9 May 1945 the following went over the airwaves:

Chapter 19 — To the Bitter End

> Achtung, achtung, Das Oberkommando
> der Wehrmacht gibt bekannt.
>
> 9 May 1945. Effective one minute past midnight the weapons on all fronts are silent. By order of the Grand Admiral the Wehrmacht has ceased its hopeless battle. Thus, nearly six years of heroic struggle have come to an end. It has brought us great victories, but also terrible losses. At the end the German Wehrmacht capitulated to overwhelming forces. With profound effort the German soldier has, true to his soldier's oath, made unforgettable sacrifices for the German people. The homeland has supported its soldiers to the extreme with heavy sacrifices. This singular effort by front and home will be properly judged by history and, in future years, will receive its final honors. Even the enemy cannot deny respect for the efforts and sacrifices of the German soldier on land, at sea, and in the air. Therefore, every soldier can lay down his weapon with pride, and in this most difficult hour of our history, work gallantly and with confidence for the eternal life of our people.
> We bow our heads in memory to those who died on the field of battle. The fallen obligate us to unconditional faithfulness, obedience, and discipline to our Fatherland bleeding from countless wounds.[6]

By the 11th of May 1945, units of the 1st and 2nd Ukrainian fronts had wiped out the last German resistance in Czechoslovakia and made contact with the Americans at Pilsen. Hostilities in Europe had officially come to an end. It had been a long and bitter war. For two boy soldiers the last three months had been especially trying. We must have wondered whether our service helped the Fatherland, or not. Most likely we had little or no impact on the events that tore apart the Fatherland. But, at least we tried. Since mid–February 1945 the Soviets had met bitter resistance among the foothills of the Sudeten Mountains and along the Wütende Neisse River; their attack was stopped by a medley of experienced combat veterans, old men, young boys, and a large contingent of foreign volunteers. During the night of 13 February, and again on 18 February, German forces counterattacked and regained some of the lost areas. Neither steady pressure nor sometimes furious Soviet attacks could pierce the German Main Line of Resistance. The MLR, leading from Häslich (County Schweidnitz), through County Jauer over Dornberg, Poischwitz, the southern edge of Jauer, Peterwitz, Kolbnitz, Herrmannsdorf, into County Goldberg, held until 6 May 1945. The main Soviet advance was westward, parallel to the line held by *Heeresgruppe Mitte*.[7] During those dark days we, among many, were there. And now, for two boy soldiers, the war had come to an end.

Postscript: Strangers in Their Own Land

So weit die rote Erde reicht,
bleibt sie vom Krieg verschont.
(As far as the red soil extends,
it will be spared from the ravages of war.)

I don't remember how often my grandmother, Preuss Oma, had whispered that old proverb. Often enough so that I still remember it today. Preuss Oma had a peasant's outlook on life. Proverbs had shaped her thinking for many years, and every so often one of them came true. The land of the red clay soil that spread along the southern slopes of the Sudeten Mountains into Czechoslovakia was indeed spared from the ravages of World War Two. Just being there had spared our families, the Thamms, the Scholzes, the Lachmanns, the Baumerts, and our dear Preuss Oma from the terrible hardship of those who had not fled the Soviet armies when they captured Jauer, our home town, on the 12th of February 1945. Those who had foolishly remained behind were brutally savaged by the Red Army. Rape and murder was a common and daily occurrence as the Soviets sought vengeance for what had been done to their land and their people by the Germans. Retribution for past sins descended on all Germans, on those who had wholeheartedly supported the Nazi regime, on those who had lived silently in quiet desperation, and on those who had actively opposed the Nazis.

With all hostilities having ceased in Europe the local Czech authorities ordered all German refugees to return to their homes. The five covered wagons of the Thamm *Trek* retraced the road over which Lothar and I had fled just a few days before. Northward the wagon train crossed the Sudeten Mountains through the Landeshuter Pass, then down into the foothills, through Bolkenhain to Jauer.

It was an uneventful voyage until the *Trek* reached Poischwitz, the village that just two weeks ago had been the forward edge of our battle area. The weather was beautiful. It was one of the finest summers even in Thamm Opa's memory. At a distance, across what had been No-Man's Land, we saw Jauer. We knew that the edges of roads and trails were saturated with antipersonnel mines. Everyone was terribly concerned that one of the horses could set off a still hidden mine. André, the Frenchman, and I led the first wagon. We led the horses by their bridles, carefully keeping to the middle of the road. Behind our wagon I saw Stutti, my favorite horse, pulling the next one. She sensed that there was grave danger; smart horses are like that. Her ears were twitching constantly, but she remained calm. Suddenly, a short distance to the right a huge fountain of earth ripped into the sky; the harsh thunder of the explosion followed immediately. It was the typical tree-shaped dirt column of an exploding German T-mine (*Tellermine*). Frightened, the horses reared up pulling André and me off our feet. Then, for a moment, everything froze in time. We calmed the horses and advanced carefully toward the location of the explosion. We had almost reached the area when two Russian soldiers in a horse-drawn wagon raced toward the site. Confused by this sudden activity we stopped near the scene of the explosion. Two other Russian soldiers and a woman lay in the field. Shrapnel had ripped the woman's stomach open. Her intestines rolled in the dirt as she twisted in pain. Near death, her left hand still clutched a net shopping bag with several loaves of bread. Near her the two severely wounded Russian soldiers lay still. All assumed that the Russians had chased the woman in an attempt to rape her; in desperation she had dashed into the mined meadow. As we stood frozen in horror, the two Russian soldiers loaded all three, and the horse-drawn wagon departed rapidly toward Jauer. Much later we heard that, incredibly, the woman had survived her terrible injuries.

Finally we arrived in Jauer. Grandfather's farm was occupied by Soviet forces. Our former farmhand, Stefan Kuznetszow, a Russian who had remained in Germany after World War One, was now the manager of Grandfather's farm. Tante Kläre departed for Lobris, only to discover her farmhouse had burned to the ground, and her husband, our Onkel Arthur, was gone.[1] She returned to Jauer to be with the rest of the Thamm family. Her faithful horse handler, André, left for France, eventually to return to Algeria. All our horses, all our wagons, with whatever the Russians wanted, were taken from us. In an instant we became impoverished. As Stutti was led away she turned her head just for a moment toward me — to say her last goodbye. This was indicative of what the future was to be. We were in Jauer, but we were strangers in our own land. While the family was away the Poles had occupied the land and had made it their own. All traces of German property ownership, all the signs over the various stores, street and road signs, and any other trace of German had vanished. In a ridiculous, bizarre way — it was almost funny — even the names over the stores torched by the Soviets sported freshly painted signs, all uniform, with red letters on white backgrounds, phony names that bore no relationship to what had been. We were told that it was their way of proving to a United Nations commission that Silesia had always been in Polish hands.

We managed to survive, but barely. Food was scarce. Lothar and I rummaged through empty houses and through the basements of ruins to bring home anything eatable. For more than a month potatoes were the only food we found. There was a shortage of salt. In desperation we used a block of salt I had found in a horse stable. Later I stole a fifty-pound bag of rape seed from a Soviet warehouse. We ground the seeds, steamed them, and pressed them to extract the oil. In autumn Preuss Oma became severely sick with typhus. Everyone thought it might have been caused by spoiled rendered animal fat from the knacker's yard; she was the only one who had eaten some of it. She developed a high fever, was delirious, and finally we loaded her on an old wooden handcart to haul her across town to an aid station. It was on the southern edge of town where a few months ago Lothar and I had assisted in loading the last of the wounded on ambulances minutes before the Soviets captured the town. In her late seventies, she was left there with little hope of survival. But the Preusses are tough. Some weeks later the family was notified that Oma was well. A nurse told us to pick her up. All of us loved her dearly and she lived another twenty years still telling her grandchildren stories about "the good old days" when the kaiser had visited Posen, or about her grandfather, the illiterate shepherd who was also a healer, and who accounted for his sheep with knots on a string.

We lived precariously in a strange town that once had been our home. We were virtual prisoners, unable to leave, and afraid to move about. It came almost as a relief when we heard rumors in August 1945 that all Germans would be deported. Early one morning Polish militia pounded on the door of Preuss Oma's apartment and ordered everyone out of the house. They told us to take only what we could carry. Once again the Thamms and the Preusses, along with every other German, fled Jauer, this time on foot. At the western end of town several members of the militia, as well as other Polish city officials, manned a roadblock. They searched us and stole whatever they wanted. Unfortunately for them there was nothing worth taking. Preuss Oma, still weak from her recent illness, Mother, Helga, and I walked westward. We slept in abandoned houses and ate whatever could be found — mostly potatoes cooked in an open fire. After trudging along for two days new orders from the Polish militia directed us to return to Jauer. Totally confused, we did. Preuss Oma, seventy-five years old, stumbled slowly along the country road, stopping every so often, afraid to sit down because she feared she would never get up. Herr Baumert, Tante Hannchen's gravedigger father, walked with us; he died from exhaustion shortly after we had once again reached Jauer. From then on someone else had to dig graves at the Protestant cemetery. In our five-day absence Preuss Oma's apartment had been taken over by a Polish family, and we found new living quarters in the back room of an abandoned grocery store on Vorwerkstrasse.

Then the Soviets rounded us up and we moved back into Grandfather's former farm. We became slave workers for the Soviet Army *Kommandantura*— Soviet headquarters. The whole Thamm family, the Scholzes, Herr and Frau Ehrlich, Mother's friends from the "olden days," were now in a labor camp guarded by Soviet soldiers. Our guard detachment — one *Starshina* (a senior sergeant) and four to six other soldiers — lived in the downstairs apartment that had been Thamm Opa's and Tante Hannchen's apartments. The guards rousted us for work call early in the morning. I am not quite certain, but was told that we were on Moscow time. That meant two or three hours before middle European time. The women milked the cows, the men tended to the horses and fed the cows. We also cleaned out the stables and every so often it was inspection time when we had to sweep the barnyard, the barns, the walks, and the streets around the farm. Initially the guards were very nervous dealing with us. The PPSh was always at the ready. The slightest move toward a guard caused the submachine gun to be aimed at the prisoner. We all became very tense. I had developed a nervous spitting habit. During one confrontation with a young guard I started to spit and he struck me in my mouth breaking several teeth. He immediately realized that I had meant him no harm and, in a touching way of apology, he wiped my face with a dirty rag he had under his belt. But the harm was done, we had no medical help available and it was more than a year later, in western Germany, before the roots of my teeth were extracted — without anesthetic.

With time the guards and the prisoners became accustomed to each other. We shared much of the food from the farm — even their tobacco. In contradiction to Communist equality there was a hierarchy in the issuing of tobacco: The common soldier received *Makhorka*, a terrible mixture of shredded tobacco stems with only minute traces of tobacco leaf; the sergeants were issued regular tobacco. Junior officers received cigarettes called *Papirossa*— half of the cigarette was filled with tobacco, the other half was a hollow tube. Senior officers carried regular cigarettes in cardboard boxes, much like those available in Western Europe. Both the sergeants and the other ranks carried their tobacco ration in their trouser pockets. Along with the tobacco they carried carefully folded bits of newspaper as cigarette paper. For cigarette paper most preferred the local army newspaper to that of *Pravda* or *Izvestia*. *Makhorka* was cut so coarse, it had to be rolled into "goat legs," paper folded akin to pipes. We, and the guards, thought that the big Communist party newspapers, *Pravda* or *Izvestia*, were unsuitable as cigarette paper; their best use was as toilet paper.

To be Soviet prisoners may sound terrible, but being under guard also had certain advantages: The Polish militia, which took great pleasure in harassing Germans could no longer badger us, and we managed to glean some food from what we produced. Grandfather, and the rest of the clan, worked the fields again just like in olden times, only now the crops belonged to the Soviets. I and my cousin Klaus, who had learned Russian rather quickly, herded cows on the meadows along the Neisse River. This was the meadow Lothar and I knew so well when Corporal Schwertfeger briefed us into his combat sector just a few months before. Although I dared not tell anyone, I even spotted the Russian mine-free alley the corporal had pointed out. Mines, or at least mine markers in Russian and German, were still everywhere. We dared not dismount from our horses. But even here modern warfare brought benefits: Every so often one of the mines would wash into the river, hit a rock, and explode. That evening we would have fresh fish to fry, and we endeared ourselves

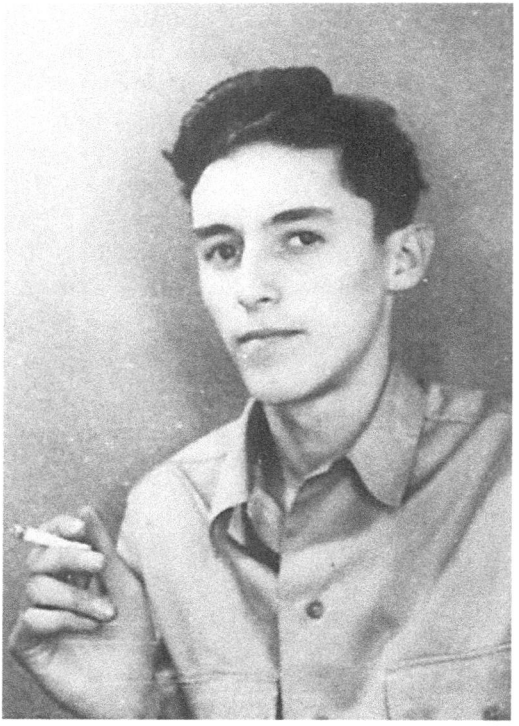

The author, trying his best to look sophisticated, in Hameln a year after Soviet imprisonment. *Author's collection.*

to the guards by sharing the fish with them — especially with Vanya, one of the guards. He preferred fish to his Soviet Army food, which he in turn gave us. Whenever Vanya had a hankering for fish he visited us at the meadow. He rode his horse into the water, scanned the river, and when he spotted a mess of fish he raised his PPSh and blasted away. This type of "fishing" always resulted in a basket full of fish.

Slave laborers are not supposed to have fun, but infrequently we did. One morning in early autumn our guards ordered several of us onto a truck to be driven into the foothills of the Sudeten Mountains. There we were told to cut firewood for the *Kommandantura*. After several days of hard work felling trees, cutting them into manageable pieces, rolling them near the logging road, and hoisting them onto the truck — an unbelievably difficult task — someone discovered already cut timber piled up neatly near the road ready to be taken. It was finely cut timber cut as coal mine shaft reinforcements for Polish mining operations in Upper Silesia. Instead of cutting trees, the guards thought it would be fun to load the already cut lumber and bring it into town. We loved it for many reasons, especially because it irritated the Poles to no end.

Just as in "the olden days" we had seeded sugar beets. In late autumn we harvested them and brought the beets to the refinery. Ivan, one of our other guards, queried us about where he could get distilling tools to make vodka. No one knew until Lothar remembered our physics laboratory at school. Ivan took us along and we searched the laboratory. He, apparently an expert moonshiner, found glass retorts, glass pipes, containers, etc., that we carried to the farm. There, with the blessings of the *Starshina* Ivan assembled a still. He then taught us how to make vodka from sugar beets, ground barley or rye, and old sourdough bread. We mixed all this with water and let it sit in a bathtub in our old laundry kitchen that had all the other needed equipment to distill alcohol — a large built-in kettle over a stove. As instructed, we allowed this brown mess to ferment, then scooped it into grain sacks. Then we placed it into our sugar beet presses to extract the juices. We allowed the juices to rest overnight so that the impurities could settle to the bottom, then Ivan poured the liquid into the retort, and the fun began.

Both Lothar and I thought Ivan to be just the greatest guy. He spoke fluent German with a pronounced Swabian dialect — we thought he was a Volga German.[2] His secret for making good vodka was minimal heat. The liquid had to simmer, not boil. He was an expert, and Lothar and I soon became his expert helpers. We watched him as he carefully placed two or three pieces of split wood on the fire. Should the fire get too hot he took one or two burning embers out, or sprayed a bit of water on the fire. As he often said, "It has to be just right." As fellow moonshiners it did not take long before the guards and Lothar and I became great friends. The suspicions that we could harm each other had long ago vanished. Now we had a common goal: endearing ourselves to the camp's leadership, and vodka was our entrée. We even experimented with making peppermint schnapps, or liqueur, by mixing readily available fresh peppermint with vodka, adding some sugar beet juice, and distilling the whole mixture again.

The winter of 1945–1946 was a bitterly cold one. Although we had cut and stolen much wood, most was destined for the *Kommandantura*. To survive we cut and burned the supporting beams from our — but no longer our — barns. We also split wood from ammunition boxes, and anything else flammable. On Christmas Eve Mother decided to cut my sister Helga's tree — the one Father had mailed in 1939 in a package from the Westwall (the Siegfried Line), where he was stationed with the Silesian 461st Infantry. At that time everyone thought that 1945 would be our last Christmas in Jauer. That Christmas tree was absolutely the finest that had ever graced a home.

Early in 1946 my father, who had been taken prisoner by the Americans in Austria, mailed a letter through the U.S. Army postal service

Page from the author's diary, 1946.

addressed to us at Jauer, Vorwerkstrasse 19. Through incredible, totally unbelievable luck, that letter reached our family at the farm that now was a Soviet *Kolchose*.³ Our family was deliriously happy to learn that he was alive. Unfortunately we had no way of telling him of our survival.

After seventeen months of incredible hardship deportation orders were posted once again. They ordered all Germans to report to the railroad station. Unfortunately, that order did not include those Germans in Soviet labor camps or working on a Soviet *Kolchose*. However, again a quirk of luck made escape possible. At the time of the deportation the Soviets were in the process of moving the *Kolchose*. Half of the guards had already been transferred, and the rest apparently did not care. In the confusion the entire family — grandfather, grandmother, aunts, and children — as well as the Ehrlich, the Baumert, and the Scholz families left. With very little on our backs we climbed into cattle cars at the railroad station.

Darkness had cast a benevolent shroud over Jauer as the train slowly rolled westward from the station toward Liegnitz. Through the open door of the cattle car we felt more than saw the so-familiar road that led from the back gate of Grandfather's farm into the fields he had tended so diligently for more than half a century. Only the faintest outlines of the barns, stables, and residence were visible, but one window, the kitchen window on the second floor, was lit, Kuznetszow, our former groom, and his family lived there in the old Hampel family apartment.

The train rolled westward; the Thamm family's farm slowly faded into darkness. I shall remember this last view of my home forever. A rumor spread as the train rumbled out of Liegnitz: The transport was going to Russia, to Siberia. As so often there was some basis for the rumor: We should have been going westward, but were rolling northward. Later we learned that the railroad bridges across the Görlitzer Neisse River had been destroyed making a slightly northward detour necessary. Eventually the train turned westward again and crossed the Görlitzer Neisse at Kohlfurt. There everyone transferred to a passenger train. To our surprise, this train was guarded by British troops. We had lost all of our belongings, but we were alive. After another day's journey we arrived in Detmold, a small town in the British Zone of Germany.

Free at last. Starving, but free.

Notes

Preface

1. *Wilson Quarterly,* (Autumn 1996). (Washington, D.C.)
2. Rolf O. Becker, *Niederschlesien 1945 — Die Flucht — Die Besetzung* (Bad Nauheim, Germany: Podzun Verlag, 1965), 242–250.
3. Albert Seaton, *The Russo-Germany War 1941-45* (Presidia Press, Novato, CA, 1993), 553.

Prologue

1. Hans von Ahlfen, *Der Kampf um Schlesien* (München: Gräfe und Unzer Verlag), 11.
2. Endearment for grandfather.

Part One: The Way It Had Been

1. Outpost Street.
2. Polish nobility.
3. The Silesian custom is to refer to people, even good friends, by their last names before their first names. In this volume, however, I have adopted the American custom of placing first names first.

Part Two: On the Home Front

Chapter 1: 1939

1. My mother's mother; *Oma* is an endearment for grandmother.
2. Military oath effective 2 August 1934 — with the death of Hindenburg.

The change of the oath from loyalty to the "Fatherland" to loyalty to the "Führer" made any opposition to Hitler high treason, a particularly wrenching dilemma for those officers of Prussian nobility steeped in 200 years of tradition of loyal service to the Fatherland.

3. Later abbreviated to GEFAZ, this phrase became a derogatory term used to describe Hitler and his follies.

Chapter 2: 1940

1. Equivalent to private first class (Pfc).
2. *Britischers* was Grandfather's term for the British he had fought in World War One.
3. Radio station.
4. *Deutsche Jugend*, of Cub Scout age.
5. *Hitler Jugend*, of Boy Scout age.
6. Later executed for attempting to kill Hitler.
7. None of Preuss Oma's sons or sons-in-law died in battle; although the Preuss boys served throughout the First World War in combat units on the Western Front. Uncle Willy served in both wars and was overrun by the Soviets in Poland in January 1945. He drove a *Panje* wagon — a small, Polish horse-drawn cart — with three Russian-speaking Waffen SS soldiers through the Soviet lines into German-held territory; they all survived. Uncle Arthur, my father's brother, died in a Siberian prison camp, but that happened well after the war had ended.
8. Day of the Eagle, the code name for the first day the Luftwaffe attacked British airfields.
9. Within the family and among friends, Grandfather never called Hitler anything else.

Chapter 5: 1943

1. Later, much later, we learned that of those 91,000 men only 5,000 ever returned. All the others died under horrible conditions in Soviet prison camps.
2. The diary was lost in the war's aftermath; only remnants remained, several of them reproduced here.
3. The propaganda minister's name for Allied raiders.
4. One estimate puts total German civilian losses during 1939–1945 at 3,640,000 and Armed Forces' deaths at 3,050,000.
5. *Sturm Abteilung*, which means Assault Unit, also known as the brown shirts.
6. German Girl Scouts.

Chapter 6: 1944

1. Flash, flash. The Supreme Command of the Armed Forces announces. This was the preamble to every public announcement from the Supreme Command — it told of glorious victories and painful defeats.

2. *Das Oberkommando der Wehrmacht gibt bekannt*, vol. 3, 1944–1945 (Osnabrück: Biblio Verlag, 1982), 118.

3. Fortifications along the English Channel coast.

4. *Das Oberkommando der Wehrmacht gibt bekannt*, vol. 3: 118.

5. The conspiracy was founded in 1939 by Count Helmuth von Moltke. Most conspirators were either Prussian nobility or German intellectuals who opposed Hitler. They met — most often on weekends — at the Moltke estate in Kreisau, Silesia. Among the many members of this circle executed were Moltke, Adam von Trott zu Solz, Count Peter York von Wartenburg, Count Friedrich Werner von der Schulenburg, and Count Claus Schenk von Stauffenberg.

The much-publicized explosion on 20 July 1944 in the *Führerbunker* at "Wolfsschanze," Hitler's headquarters in Rastenburg, East Prussia, was just another failed attempt to kill the Führer. The consequences of that failure were devastating. Few Kreisauer Kreis conspirators survived that debacle to tell their side. The lucky ones were summarily executed by firing squad — some by fellow conspirators — others committed suicide; most died the horrible death of hanging or garroting at Plötzensee Prison near Berlin. Nazi newspapers published the names of fifty; their immediate families were placed in death camps where many perished.

6. *Schutz Staffel*, which means Protective Squadron, the original black-shirts, later organized as elite combat divisions.

7. *Geheime Staats Polizei*, which means Secret State Police.

8. *Das Oberkommando der Wehrmacht* 3: 194.

9. Another of Goebbels' propaganda ploys: To save his family from Nazi retribution, Rommel was forced to commit suicide for his supposed involvement in the plot to kill Hitler.

Part Three: Götterdämmerung (Apocalypse)

Chapter 8: The Omen

1. A section of the Eastern Front.

2. *Das Oberkommando der Wehrmacht* 3: 400.

3. A walking encirclement entailed fighting on all sides while "advancing to the rear."

4. *Das Oberkommando der Wehrmacht* 3: 405–406.

Chapter 9: Distant Thunder

1. Karl Dönitz, *Zehn Jahre und Zwanzig Tage* (Bonn: Athenaeum Verlag, 1958),431.
2. *Das Oberkommando der Wehrmacht* 3: 427.
3. Peoples' Militia.
4. Becker..., *Niederschlesien*, 242.
5. Uncle.
6. Combat commander.
7. *Das Oberkommando der Wehrmacht* 3: 434.
8. *Oberkommando der Wehrmacht*, which means High Command of the Armed Forces.
9. *Das Oberkommando der Wehrmacht* 3: 438–439.

Chapter 10: Flight

1. *Das Oberkommando der Wehrmacht* 3: 442–443.
2. Becker, *Niederschlesien...*, 242–250.
3. City hall.
4. City hall restaurant, usually one of the best eating places in town.
5. A word for Americans, almost an endearment.
6. An old word for a country road.
7. The new market, also called the "horse traders' market"; the old market was in the city hall square.
8. The German abbreviation for *Jagdbomber*—ground attack aircraft.
9. The German antitank rocket, a one-shot, throwaway weapon with a large warhead. Hand-launched, it consisted of a heavy shaped-charge warhead and a small pipe filled with solid rocket fuel. Affixed to the pipe were four stabilizing tail fins. This crude device was stuck into an aluminum pipe containing the launch propellant, the firing mechanism, and a simple folding sight. The weapon became armed when the sight was unfolded and the trigger was released. After launching the weapon you threw the launcher away. As crude as this weapon was, it punched a 2–2½ inch hole through the most heavily armored part of a tank. As far as I know, no other nation had such a powerful hand-held antitank weapon—it was a version of the American bazooka, but far superior to it.
10. An old sergeant in the German 100th Jäger Division called the *Panzerfaust* the hallelujah weapon because "if you don't have one, it's hallelujah."
11. The nickname came from their symbol of authority, a crescent-shaped, cast aluminum shield with the German eagle and the word *Feldpolizei*, which hung across the chest suspended from a heavy silver-colored linked chain.

Chapter 11: Retreat into the Sudeten Mountains

1. Large squares of cotton cloth used in lieu of socks. They are actually quite comfortable to wear, better than socks.
2. Becker, *Niederschlesien*, 242–250.
3. Hans von Ahlfen, *Der Kampf um Schlesien* (München: Gräfe und Unzer Verlag), 149–152.
4. *Ibid.*
5. *Ibid.*
6. *Ibid.*
7. *Das Oberkommando der Wehrmacht* 3: 457.
8. *Ibid.*

Chapter 14: Frontline Duty

1. *Das Oberkommando der Wehrmacht* 3: 554.
2. Hans von Ahlfen, *Der Kampf um Schlesien*, 160–161.

Chapter 15: The "Forgotten Front"

1. A derogatory term for members of the Nazi party; their brown uniforms had much gold braiding.

Chapter 16: The Russian Boy

1. Von Ahlfen, *Der Kampf um Schlesien*, 159.
2. Low-level infantry.
3. Von Ahlfen, *Der Kampf um Schlesien*, 159–169.
4. Cesare Salmaggi and Alfredo Pallavisini, *2194 Days of War: An Illustrated Chronology of the Second World War* (New York: Gallery Books, W.H. Smith, Publishers, Inc., 1988),698.

Chapter 17: "Routine" Patrol

1. A wound serious enough for even a German soldier to be discharged — to go home.

Chapter 18: Ah, Natascha

1. Words from an ancient song.
2. Hip bath.
3. Farmer's bread.

Chapter 19: To the Bitter End

1. Salmaggi and Pallavisini, *2194 Days of War*, 798.
2. Degrading the fighting will, a capital offense.
3. *Das Oberkommando der Wehrmacht* 3: 562.
4. *Ibid.*
5. *Ibid.*
6. *Ibid.*
7. Becker, *Niederschlesien*, 242–250.

Postscript: Strangers in Their Own land

1. No one knows the suffering my Uncle Arthur had to endure. In March of 1945 he and 1900 other men and 411 women were shipped in cattle cars to a camp north of the Arctic Circle near the Barents Sea. Eleven years later we learned from a fellow prisoner that Uncle Arthur died at Kandalakscha Camp 1513, near Murmansk.
2. German farmers from the Swabian and Baden principalities had migrated to the Volga region during czarist days.
3. Collective farm.

Index

Aachen 66
Der Adler 19
Adlertag 29, 170
Afrika Korps 37, 42
Albania 33, 37
Alte Schule (Jauer) 14
Altenbuchen 120, 142, 143, 145, 156
Altmark (merchant ship) 26
Altreichenau 101, 105, 120
Ambulance trains 70–74, 78–79, 81, 91–92
André (French POW) 160, 161
Arnold, Herr 2
Assault Unit *see* Sturm Abteilung
Atrocities 2–3, 19, 21, 22, 63, 84, 85, 99, 135, 160
Aulhausen Hospital 28
Ausgebombte 49
Austria 29, 40, 69, 73
Axmann, Arthur 26

Bahnhofstrasse (Jauer) 21
Balkans 51
Baltic 43, 59, 62, 65, 77, 78
Baranow bridgehead 77
Baumert, Herr 43, 162
Baumert, Kurt 34
Baumert family 88, 159, 166
Bautzen 117
Bavaria 29, 73, 89, 140, 156
Benelux countries 28
Berlin 33, 39, 56, 97, 127, 131, 153, 154, 155
Berlin-Magdeburg rail line 73
Bienenkörbe 11
Bismarck 34
Blackouts 22, 56
Blitzkrieg 78, 81

Bohemia 19, 96
Bolkenhain 90, 96, 105, 106, 111, 115, 120, 126, 127, 134, 135, 143, 144, 145, 160
Bolkoburg 105, 106
Breslau 6, 55, 78, 97, 126, 151, 155
Breslau-Jauer rail line 73
Breslau-Liegnitz-Glogau battle sector 85
Brieg 87
Brown Shirts *see* Sturm Abteilung
Brückner, General 118
Bulgaria, capitulation 62
Bundesministerium für Vertriebene 2
Bürgerbräukeller 60
Bund Deutscher Mädchen 74, 96, 170
Bunzlau 87
Burkhard, Pfc. 113

Carpathian Mountains 77
Chaindogs *see* Feldpolizei
Chamberlain, Neville 28, 29
Chaussee see Liegnitzer Chaussee
Christmas 24, 31, 38, 41, 45, 53–54, 66, 68–69, 165
Churchill, Winston 28, 29, 33
Clergy 79, 84
Combat Sector Jauer 121
Communism in Spain 19
Communists 25, 27
Croatian volunteers 118
"Cross of Motherhood" *see* "Mother's Cross"
Czechoslovakia 9, 19, 29, 68, 81, 98, 99, 120, 151, 155, 157, 159

Day of the Eagle *see* Adlertag
Denmark 28
Detmold 167

Deutsche Jugend see German Youth Movement
Dnepropetrovsk 51
Dniepr River 51
Dönitz, Karl, Admiral 154
Dornberg 157
Dresden 73, 78, 97, 117, 156

East Prussia *see* Prussia, East
Eastern Front 1, 6, 39, 49, 51, 52, 55, 62, 70–71, 79, 82, 110, 128
Ehingen Hospital 28
Ehrenberg, Ilja 84, 147
Ehrlich, Herr and Frau 162, 166
Elbe River 135, 156
England 29
Estonian Infantry Division (20th) 126

Faustpatrone see Panzerfaust
Feldpolizei 95, 97, 172
Finland, capitulation 62
France 28
Frederick the Great 10, 21, 61
French POWs 85
Friedenskirche (Jauer) 36, 37, 38, 53
Friedhof (Jauer) 14, 15
Fussell, Paul 1

GEFAZ 22, 127, 170
Gefreiter 24, 26, 31, 33, 34, 38, 47, 51
Geheime Staats Polizei see Gestapo
German Air Force: Panzer Division Hermann Göring, a.k.a. Parachute-Panzer Division Hermann Göring 47; 6th Battery, 388th Heavy Antiaircraft Section, 45
German Army: Army Group Center (*Mitte*) 51, 97, 98, 158; Army Group South 51; 1st Army 28; 4th Tank Army 42; 6th Army 42; 17th Army 97; VIII Korps 98; XI Korps 42; LIX Korps 135; 100th Jäger (Light Infantry) 90, 97, 109, 172; 208th Division 135; 269th Infantry (Hamburg) 90; *Volkssturm* 87, 106, 131; *Volkssturm* Battalion Jauer/ 83, 90
German Boy Scouts 96, 105
German Girl Scouts *see Bund Deutscher Mädchen*
German invasion of Denmark and Norway 26
German invasion of France and Benelux countries 28

German invasion of Russia 38
German Main Line of Resistance *see* MLR
German minorities in Poland 21
German occupation of Hungary and Rumania 52
German Refugee Ministry *see Bundesministerium für Vertriebene*
German State Railway 72, 155
German surrender 157
German Youth Movement 26, 34, 170
Gestapo 61, 171
Glogau 97, 126
Goebbels, Joseph 21–22, 28, 32, 34, 43, 45, 51, 52, 55, 59, 148, 153, 154, 171
Göring, Hermann 29, 34, 49, 154
Görlitz 97, 135
Görlitz-Schwedt line 97
Goldap 63
Goldberg 87, 97, 158
Goldenau 156
Gomel 53
Graudenz 78
Great Depression 27
Great War *see* World War I
Greece 33, 37
Grete 37, 43, 49, 59, 65
Grünberg, Herr 53
Gumbinnen 63

Häslich 157
Hallelujah weapon *see Panzerfaust*
Heavy Antiaircraft Artillery Section (388th), 6th Battery 45
Heeresgruppe Mitte see German Army Group Center
Heimatschuss 140, 142
Henry II, Polish Duke 9
Hermann, Ursula ("Uschi") 32–33, 57, 66, 67, 68
Hermannsdorf 158
Hess, Rudolf 33, 34, 37
Himmler, Heinrich 34
Hindenburg 169
Hirschberg 155
Hirschberger Pass 155
Hitler, Adolf 19, 21, 22, 24, 25, 26, 29, 34, 38; assassination attempts, 60, 62, 171; birthday celebrations, 26–27, 37, 57, 152; suicide, 126, 154
Hitler Jugend see Hitler Youth Movement
Hitler Youth Movement 26–27, 50, 59, 64, 87, 170

Index

Hohenelbe 156
Hör zu! 14
Hoth, Hermann, Gen. 43
Hungary 52, 62

Italian military 29, 32, 33, 37, 42, 47, 50, 51

Jagdbomber 172
Jauer 5, 9, 10, 14, 24, 38, 40, 53, 55, 81, 87, 97, 99, 111, 114, 121, 157, 158, 160, 162
Jauer-Goldberg line 97
Jauer non-commissioned officers' school 79, 84
Jauersche Würstel 9
Jauersches Stadtblatt 28
Jauerwagen 11

Katzbach Mountains 97
Katzbach River 10
Kaulbach's, (Restaurant) 34, 49
Kiev 51, 53
Kohlfurt 167
Kolbnitz 158
Krakow 78, 79
Krebs, General 154
Kreisauer Kreis 60, 61, 171
Kremenchug 51
Kronau 63
Kursk, Battle of 43, 49
Kuznetszow, Stefan 160, 167

Lachmann family 88, 159
Landeshut 98, 99, 120, 140, 144, 156
Landeshuter Pass 155, 160
Lauban 98, 134
Legion Condor 19
Lehngut 13
Liegnitz 9, 82, 85, 86, 97, 167
Liegnitzer Chaussee 90, 91
Linz 45, 49
Little Erich 115, 116, 119, 126, 138, 151
Lobris 83, 85, 161
Lötzen County 63
London Blitz *see Adlertag*
Lotte 37
Lower Silesia *see* Silesia, Lower
Luftwaffe 29, 87, 126, 170

Maginot Line 28, 31
Mährisch-Ostrau gap 135
Maltsch 82

Mannstein, Field Marshal von 43
Maria Theresa, Empress of Austria 10
Max and Moritz 37
Mennonites 11
Military oath 21, 169–170
MLR 78, 118, 157
Model, Walther, Field Marshal 43
Moltke, Count Helmuth von 171
Mongols, Battle Against 9
Moravia 19
"Mother's Cross" 26

NCO School Jauer *see* Jauer non-commissioned officers' school
Napoleon 38
Natascha 142–150, 152, 153
Natzmer, General von, 98
Nazi Party 1, 14, 20, 24, 25, 26, 27, 34, 35, 38, 39, 50, 57, 60, 61, 65, 90, 91, 96, 115
Neisse River 9, 32, 63, 91, 97, 114, 131, 157, 163, 167
Nemmersdorf 63
Neumarktstrasse (Jauer) 38
Niederschlesien *see* Silesia, Lower
Normandy invasion 59, 60
Norway 26, 28, 55

Oberseeberg 34
Oder River 1, 67, 68, 77, 79, 81, 83, 84, 97, 109
OKW 84, 97, 117
Operation *Adlertag* see *Adlertag*
Oppeln 135

Panzerarmee (4th) see German Army (4th Tank Army)
Panzerfaust 82, 94, 109, 118, 129, 152, 172
Paulus, *General* 42
Pearl Harbor 38
Pekhota 135, 136–137
Peterwitz 158
Pferdemarkt 38
Pilsen 157
Pinne 34, 35
Plötzensee Prison 171
Poischwitz 131, 133, 135, 157, 160
Poland 19, 20, 21–22, 23, 35, 67, 82, 109
Posen 19, 35, 78
Preuss, Oma 19, 24, 29, 53, 142, 159, 161, 162
Preuss, Opa 19
Preuss, Willy 34–35

Preuss family 19
Pröst, Herr 50, 52, 56
Prussia 10, 13, 82
Prussia, East 1, 63

Rastenburg 171
Rationing 23, 53, 56, 57, 101
Rathskeller Restaurant 10
Refugees 78, 81, 89, 101, 160
Reichard, Colonel 84
Reichsender Breslau 26
Rhine-Marne Canal 28
Ritter, Herr 2
Rommel, Erwin, Field Marshal 37, 59, 63, 171
Roosevelt, Franklin D. 11
Rössel County 63
Rübezahl 11
Rumania 52, 62

Saarbrücken 28
Saarlautern 68
Sagan 87
St. Martin Kirche 38
Scharnhorst 55
Scholz, Lothar 13, 32, 55, 57, 64, 65, 66, 67, 68, 70, 87, 88, 89, 90–92, 94, 96, 98, 100, 101, 105, 111, 113–114, 119, 120, 153, 155, 156, 161, 164–165
Scholz, Susi 13, 64, 65–66, 67, 68, 142, 145
Schörner, General 138, 151
Schulenburg, Count Friedrich Werner, von der 171
Schulzenwalde 63
Schurz, Lance Corporal 82
Schutz Staffel 35, 61, 118, 171
Schutzbrief 29
Schwedt *see* Görlitz-Schwedt line
Schweidnitz 97, 157
Schweiseingen 28
Schwertfeger, Corporal 111, 115, 116, 122–124, 126, 129, 130, 134, 135, 139, 151, 163
Seaton, Albert 3
Seille 28
Sergeant "One-Eye" 107–110, 111, 120, 127, 128, 151, 153, 155
Sicily 47
Siegfried Line 22, 26
Silesia 1, 5, 9,10, 28, 65, 77, 82, 97, 135, 147, 161
Silesia, Lower 2–3, 5, 84, 87, 99, 109, 126
Silesia, Upper 62, 98, 125, 135, 164

Silesian dialect 10, 16
Silesian Infantry Regiments 21; 83rd 11, 20; 154th 10, 12; 461st (Reserve)11, 20, 26, 28, 165
Social Democrats 25
Solz, Adam von Trott, zu 171
Sommerfeld training area 20
Sommersingen 16
Sorau 135
Soviet Army: Central Front 51; First Ukrainian Front, 2, 121, 135, 157; Fourth Ukrainian Front, 135; Second Ukrainian Front, 157; Southwest Front, 51; Steppe Front, 51; Ukrainian Front, 98
Soviet winter offensive 35, 38, 40
SS *see Schutz Staffel*
Stalingrad, Battle of 42, 51
Stauffenberg, Count Claus Schenk, von 171
Steinau-on-Oder 79, 83, 84
Striegau 97, 134, 135
Sturm Abteilung 170
Stutti 20, 37, 40, 43, 49, 59, 62, 65, 78, 88, 160
Submarines, German *see* U-boats.
Sudeten Mountains 9, 13, 68, 90, 96, 97, 98, 99, 105, 109, 120, 125, 131, 135, 157, 159, 160, 164

Thamm, Arthur, *Uncle* 1, 12, 21, 53, 83, 85, 161, 174
Thamm, Erna, *Mother* 19, 22, 35, 64, 88, 100, 101, 142, 162, 165
Thamm, Erwin, *Father* 14, 20–22, 23, 24, 26; wounded on Western front 28–29; 35, 38, 41, 45, 48, 165
Thamm, Gerhard, *Uncle* 20, 21, 34, 40
Thamm, Gisela, *Cousin* 85
Thamm, Hannchen, *Aunt* 162
Thamm, Helga, *Sister* 40, 70, 101, 141, 144, 162
Thamm, Hermann (Opa), *Grandfather* 6, 12, 13, 22, 24–25, 32, 38, 39, 43, 49, 160, 162
Thamm, Kläre, *Aunt* 53, 83, 85, 100, 101, 161
Thamm, Otto, *Uncle* 12
Thuringia 98
Tobruk 33
Torgau-on-the-Elbe 126
Trautenau 120, 142, 156
Treks 2, 81, 88, 99, 101, 120, 156, 160

Trenker, Sebastian 141, 148
Tschenstochau 79

U-boats 39, 47
Unteroffizierschule Jauer *see* Jauer non-
  commissioned officers' school
Upper Silesia *see* Silesia, Upper
Urach Hospital 28

Versailles Diktat 14
Vistula Front 77, 78, 79
Vitebsk 53
Volksgasmaske 22
Vorwerk 11
Vorwerkgut 19, 20
Vorwerkstrasse (Jauer) 9, 13, 21, 32, 166

Waffen SS, 87 170
Wagner, General 90
Wahlstatt 9

Walter, Anna 2
Wartenburg, Count Peter York, von 171
Warthe River 35
Wehrkraftzersetzung 152
Wehrmacht 2, 69, 131, 157
Western Front 1, 23, 26, 27, 59, 60, 63, 170
Westwall *see* Siegfried Line
Witzleben, General von 28
"Wolfsschanze" 170
World War I 6, 12, 19, 22, 26, 29, 34, 51, 63, 72, 160, 171
Wütende Neisse *see* Neisse River

Xylander, General von 97

Yugoslavia 33, 37

Zhitomir 53
Zobten 98

www.ingramcontent.com/pod-product-compliance
Ingram Content Group UK Ltd.
Pitfield, Milton Keynes, MK11 3LW, UK
UKHW042015140426
5217IPUK00015B/1181